Beautiful Face

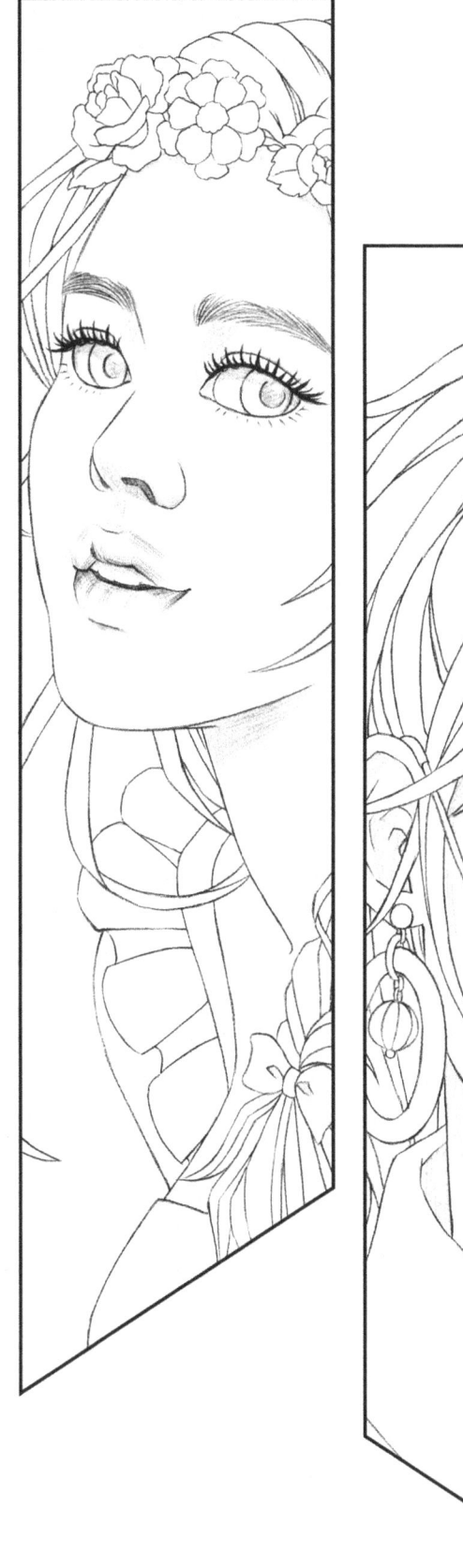
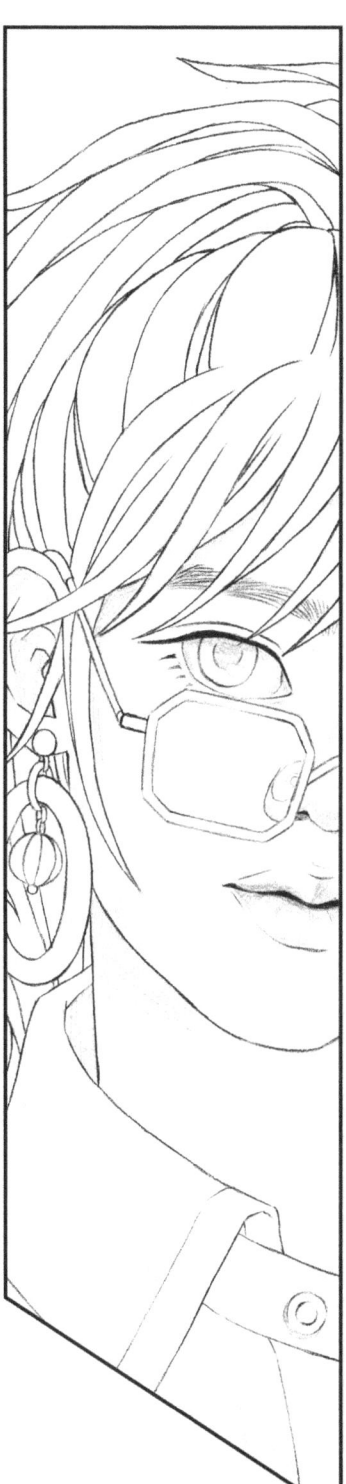
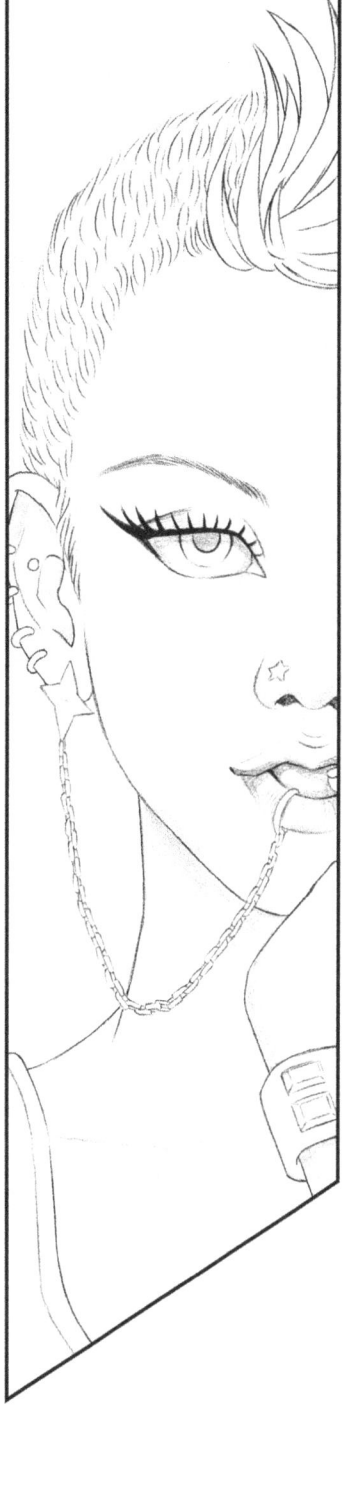
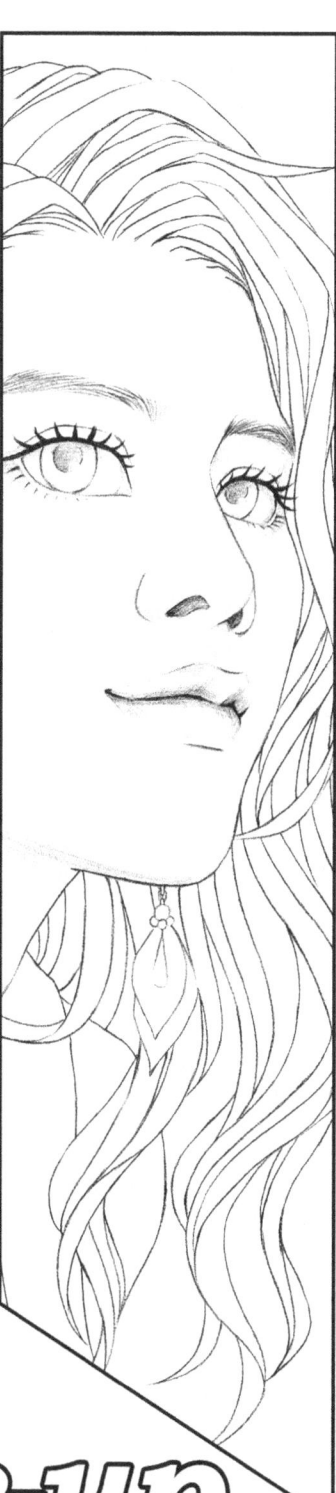

30 portrait drawings

for *Make-up* Coloring

ISBN-13 9798592082740
First published in United States in 2021
All artworks are made by Queenie Wong.
Wonger0050@yahoo.com.hk
Copyright 2021 by Queenie Wong
All rights reserved.
No part of this book may be reproduced in any form for commercial used without written permission from the author.

Image number shown at the back of the page

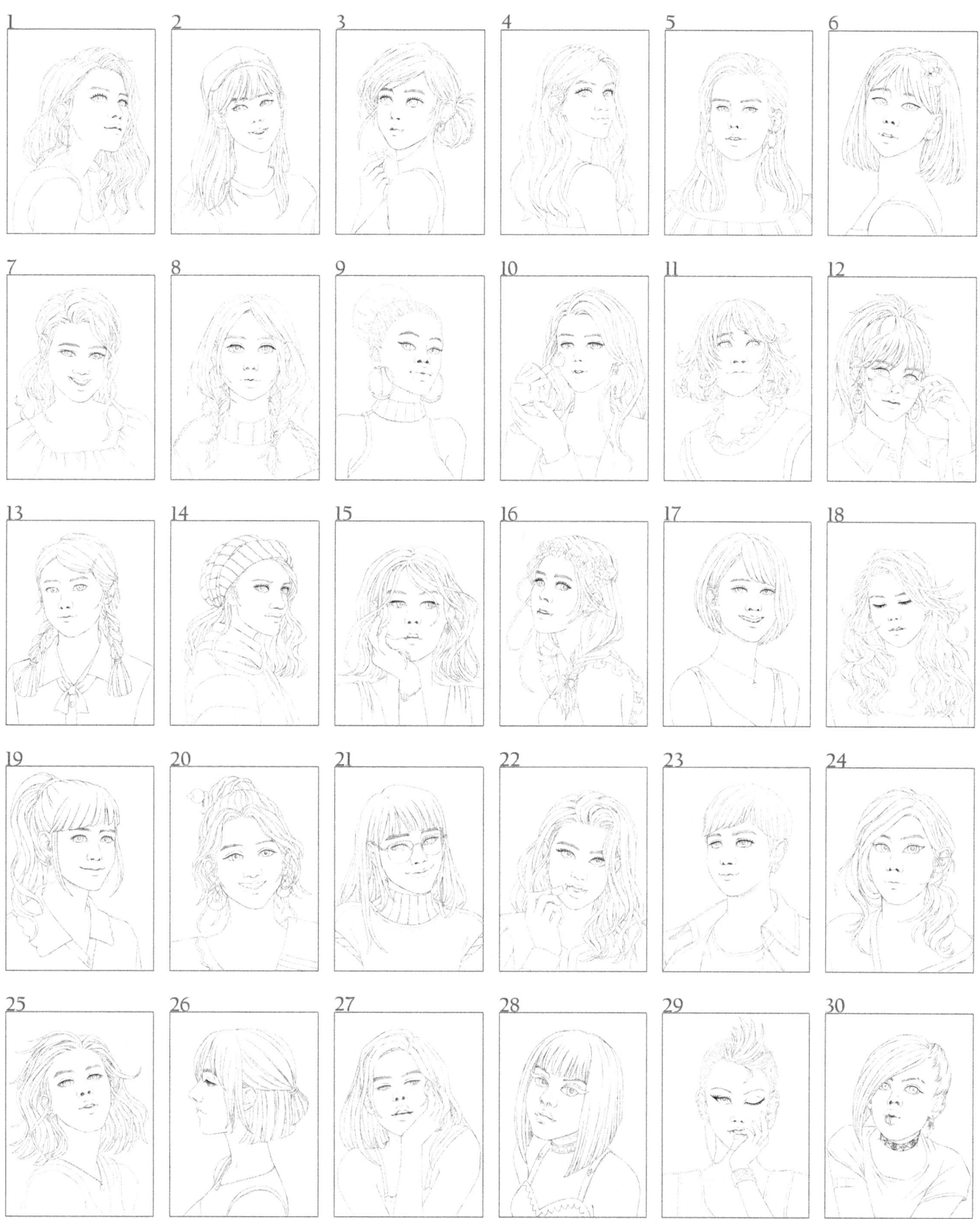

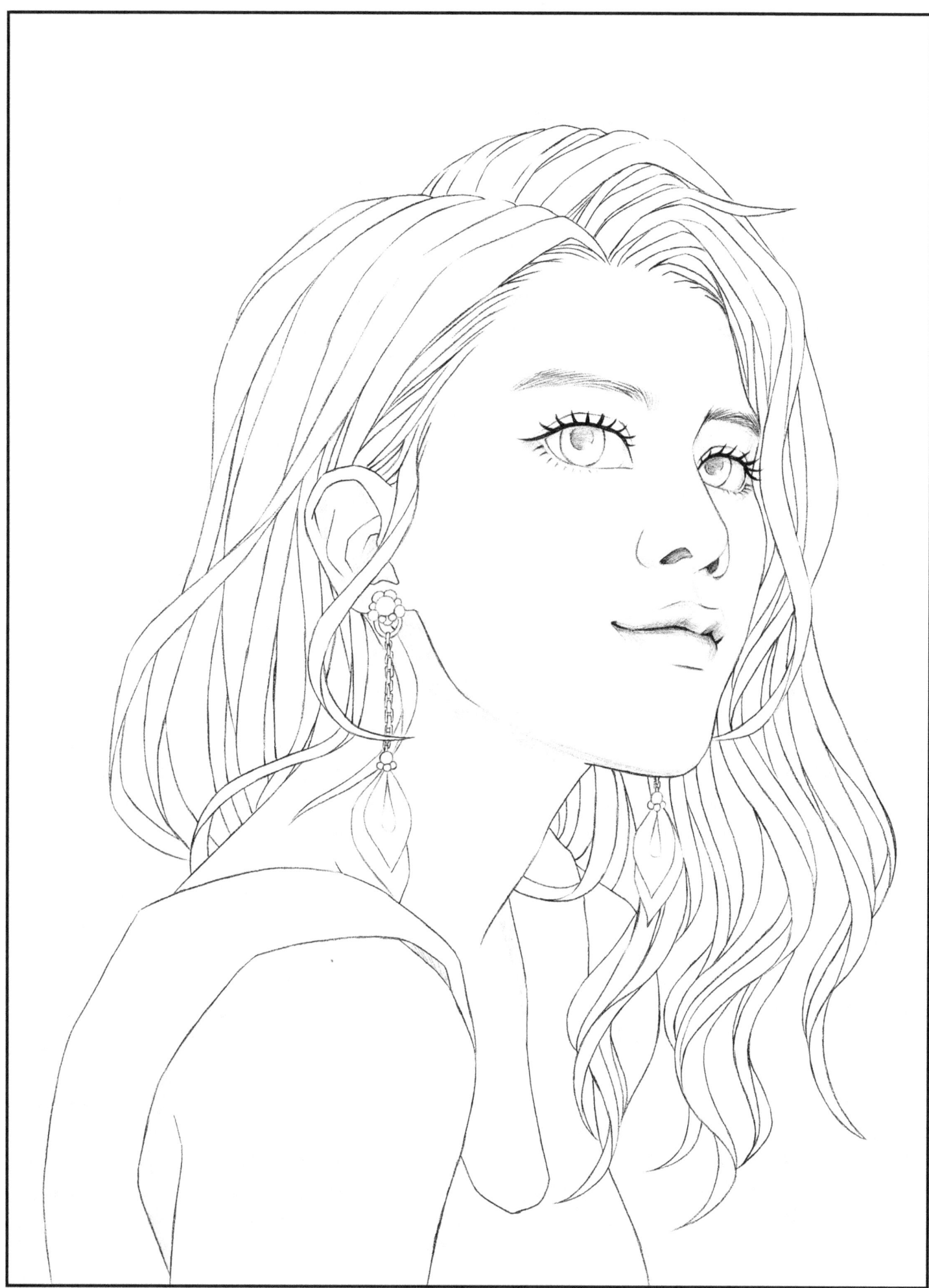

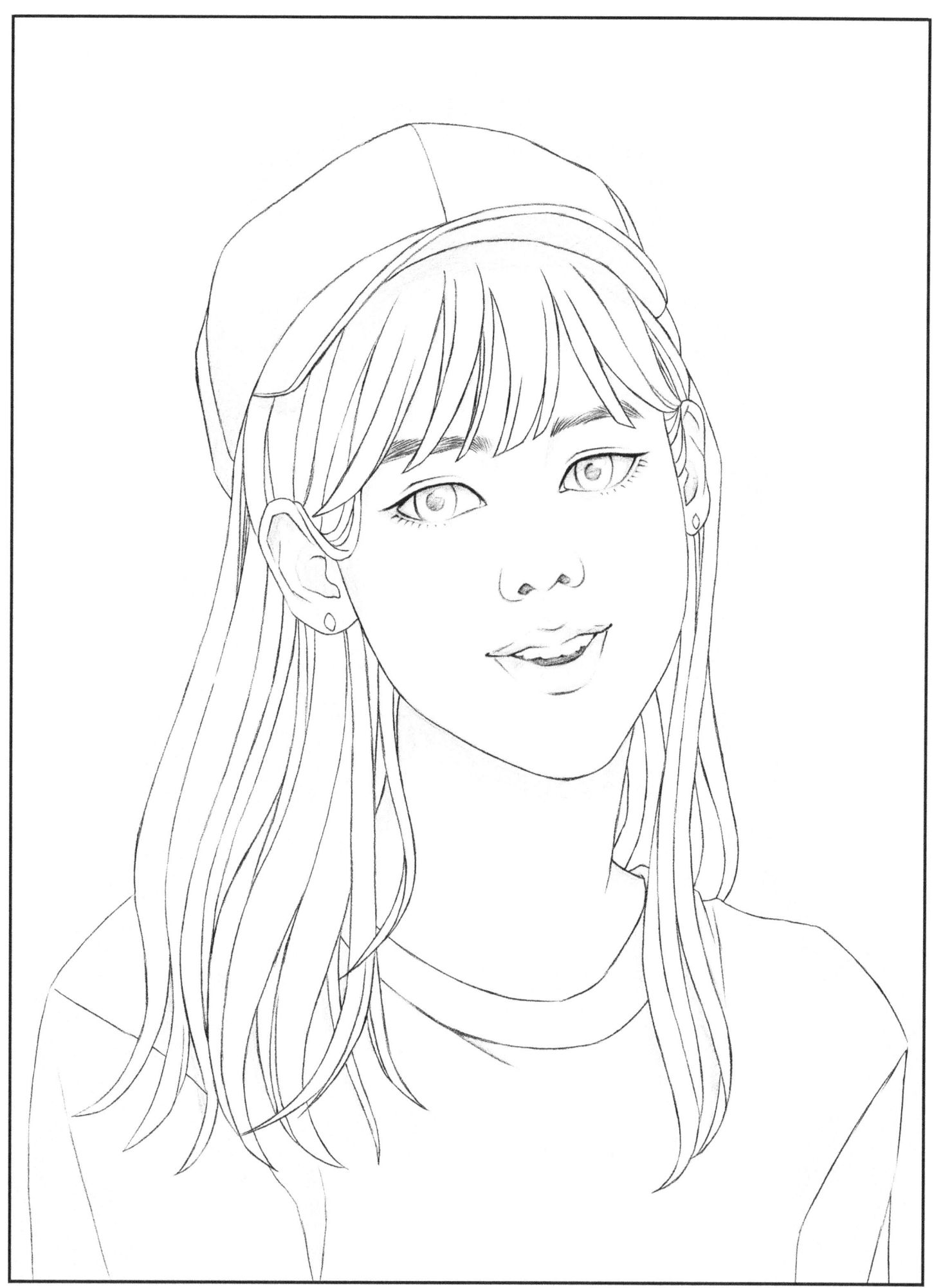

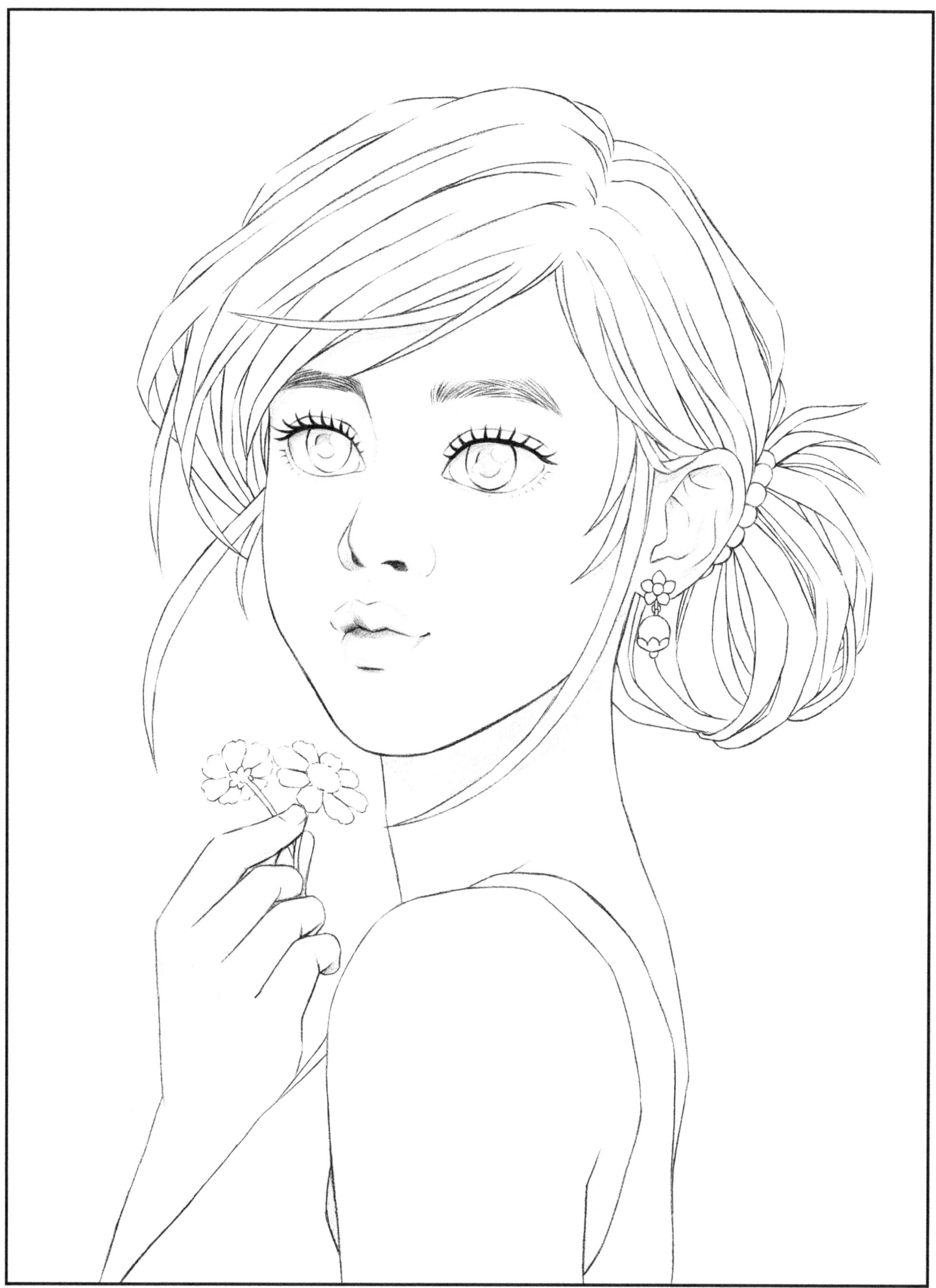

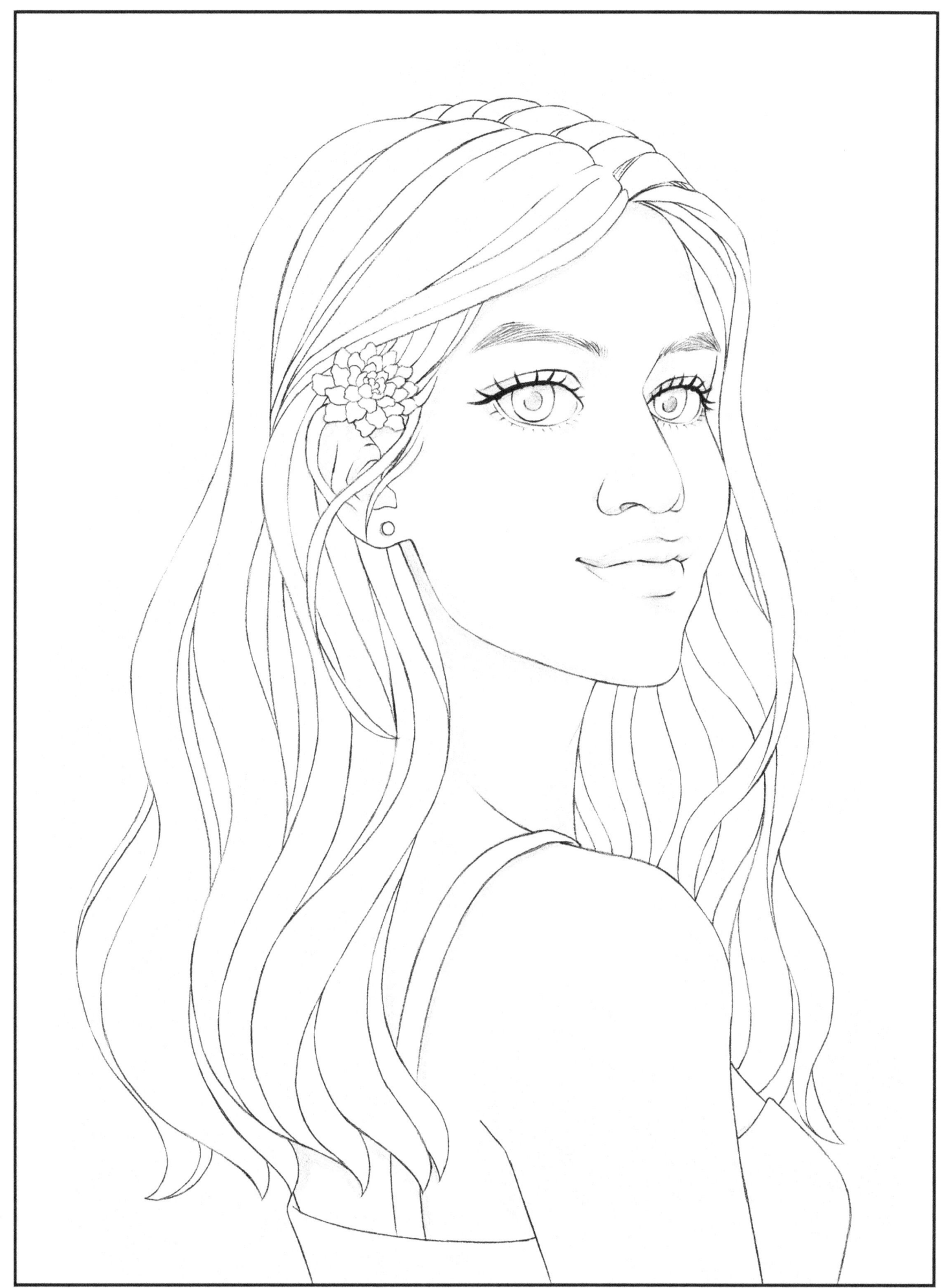

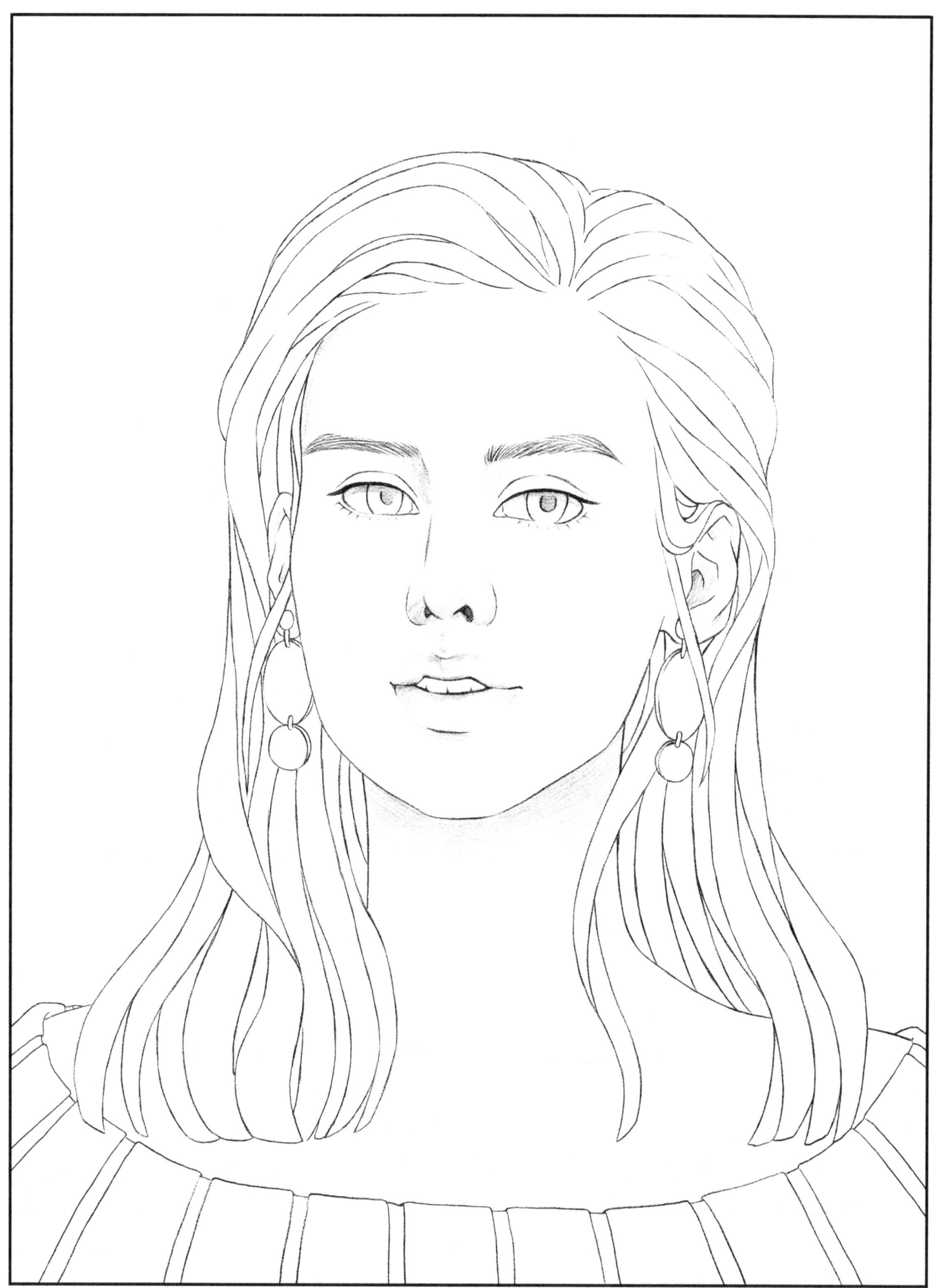

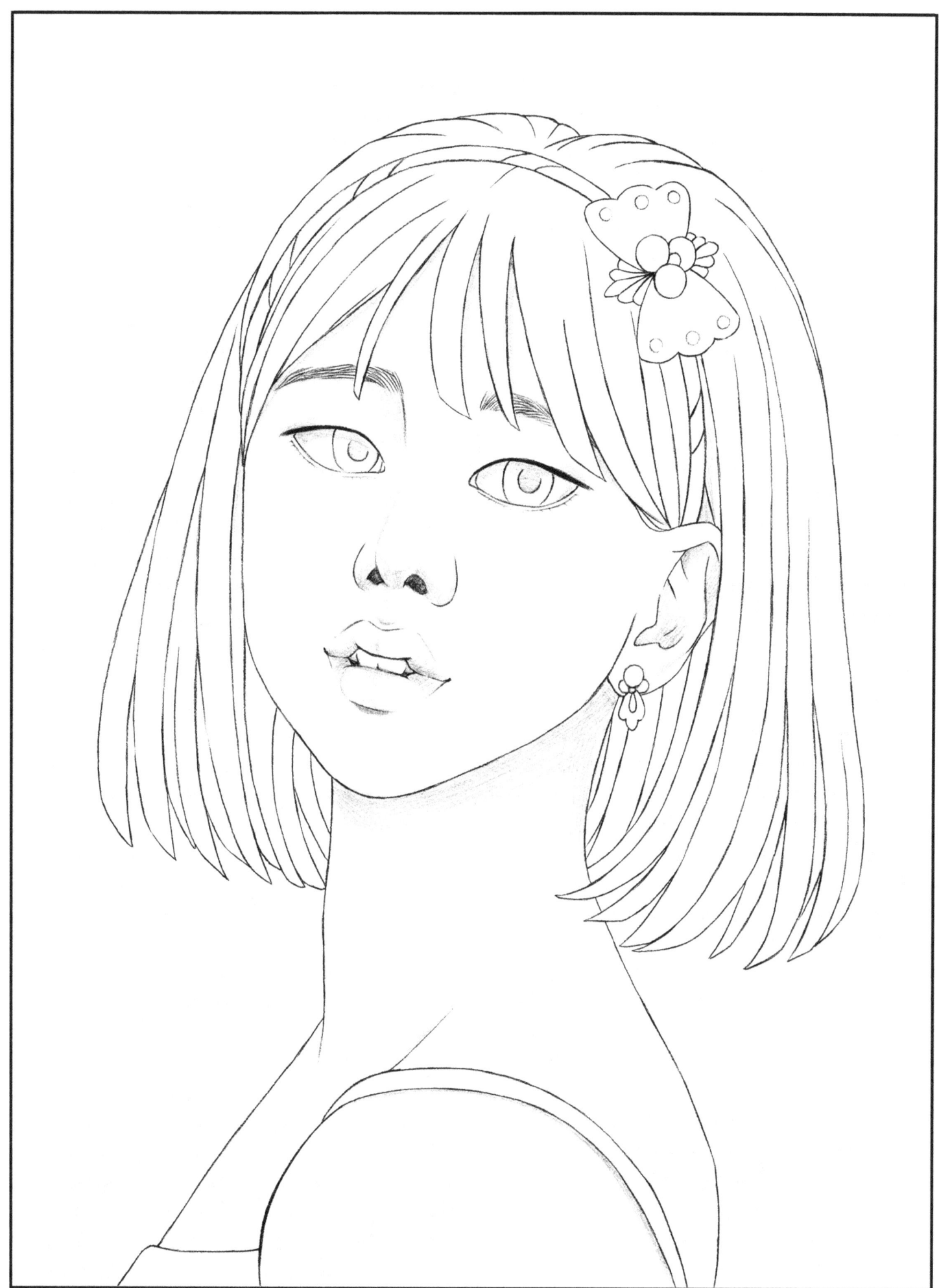

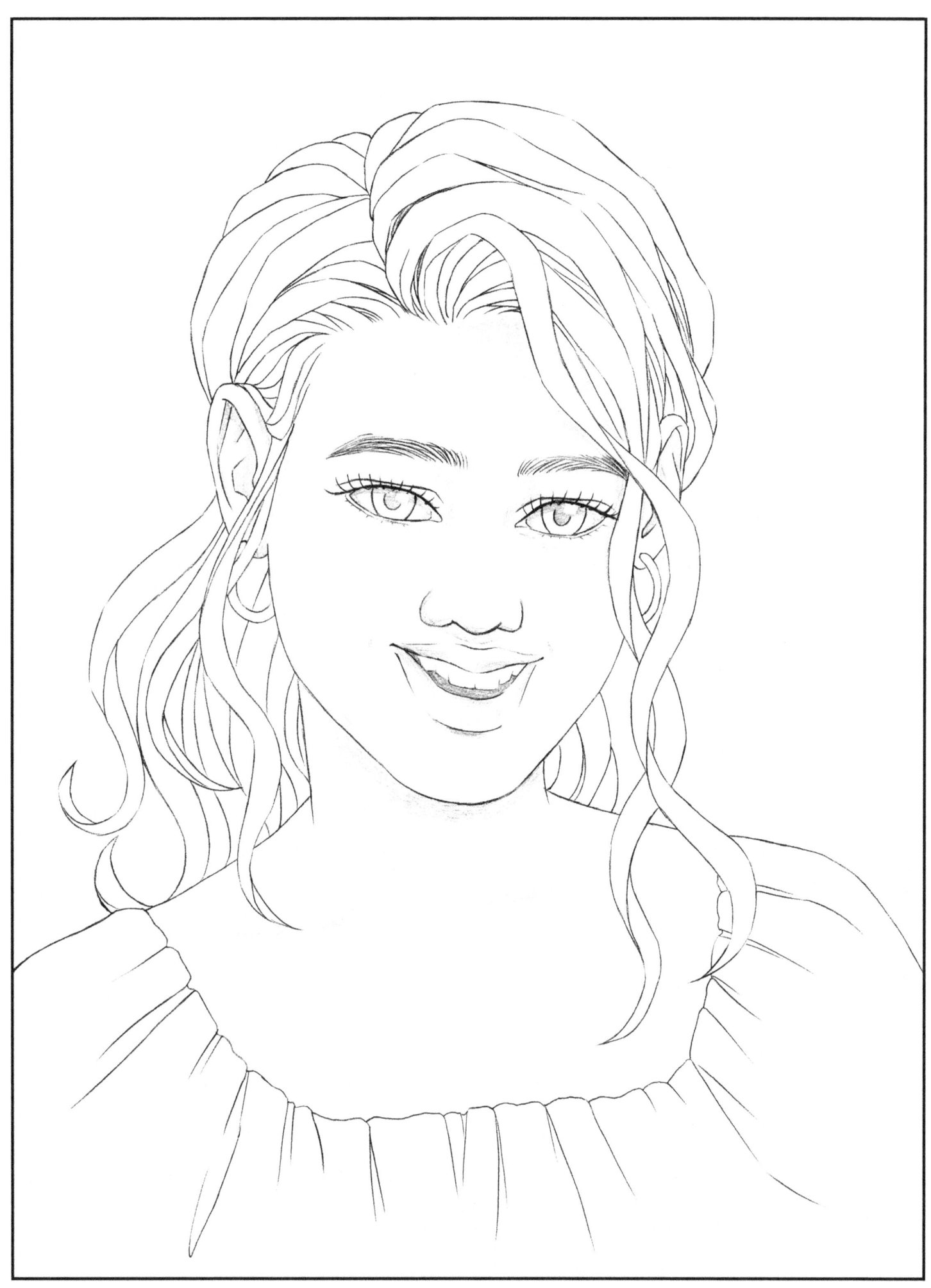

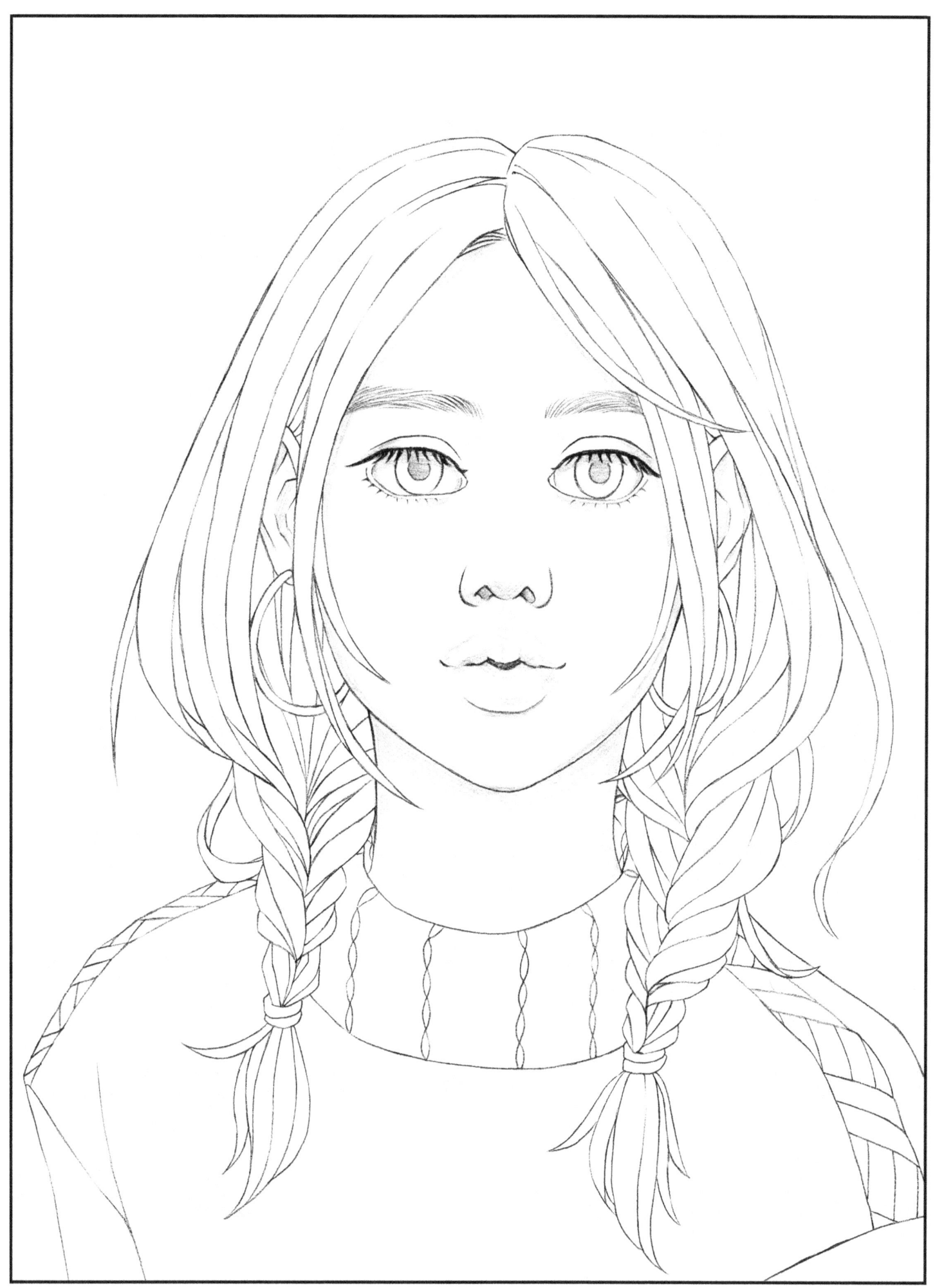

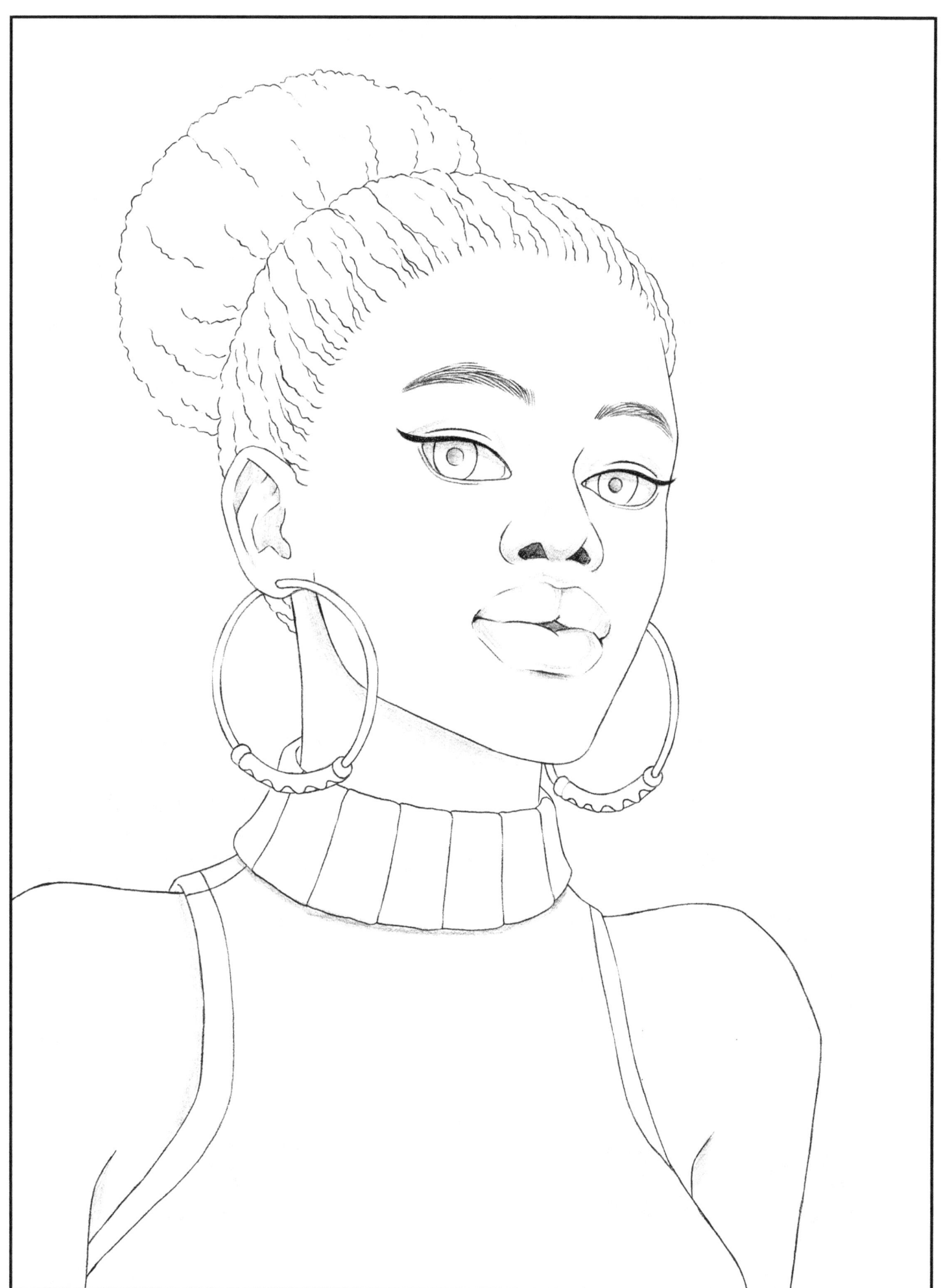

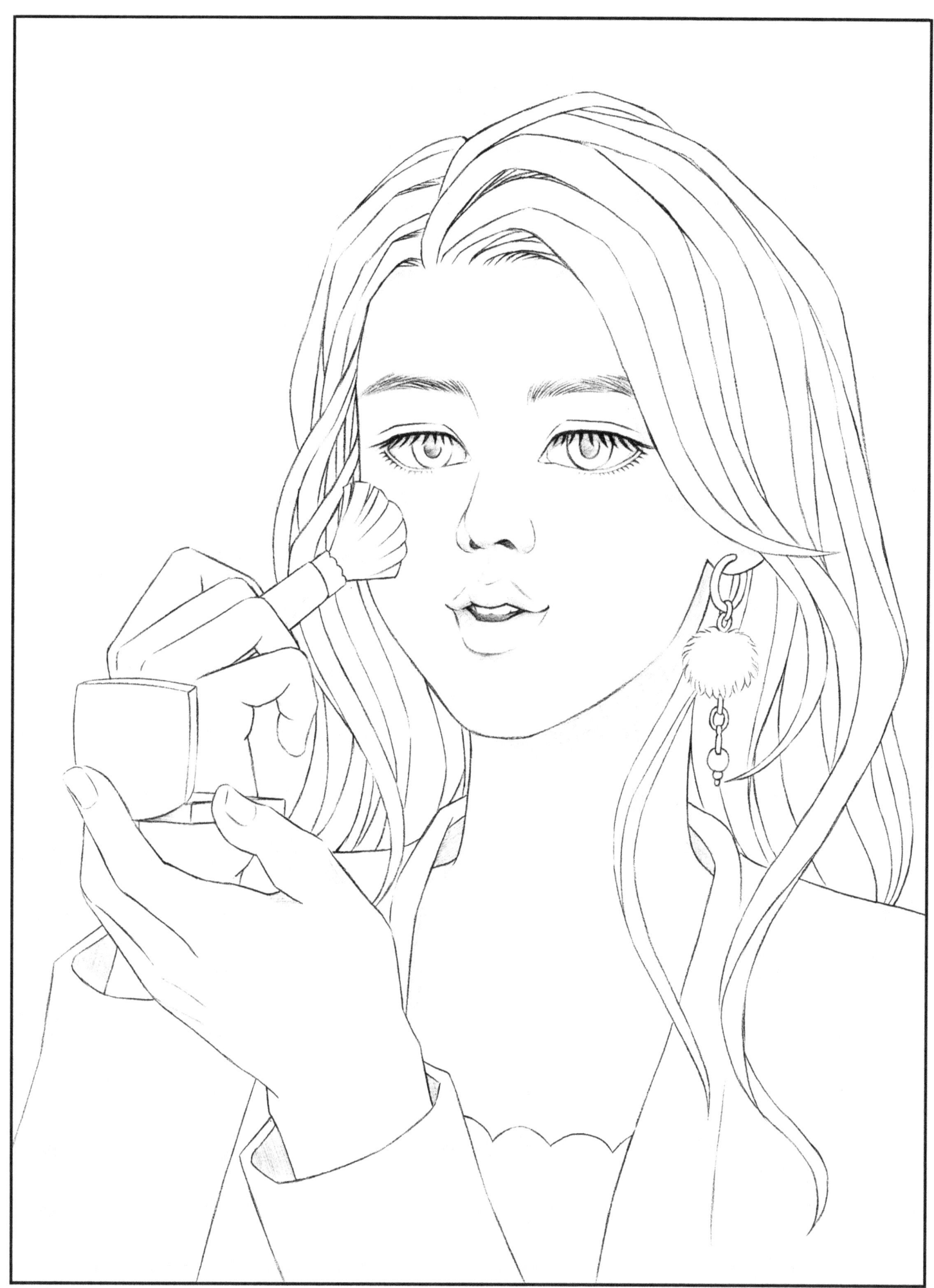

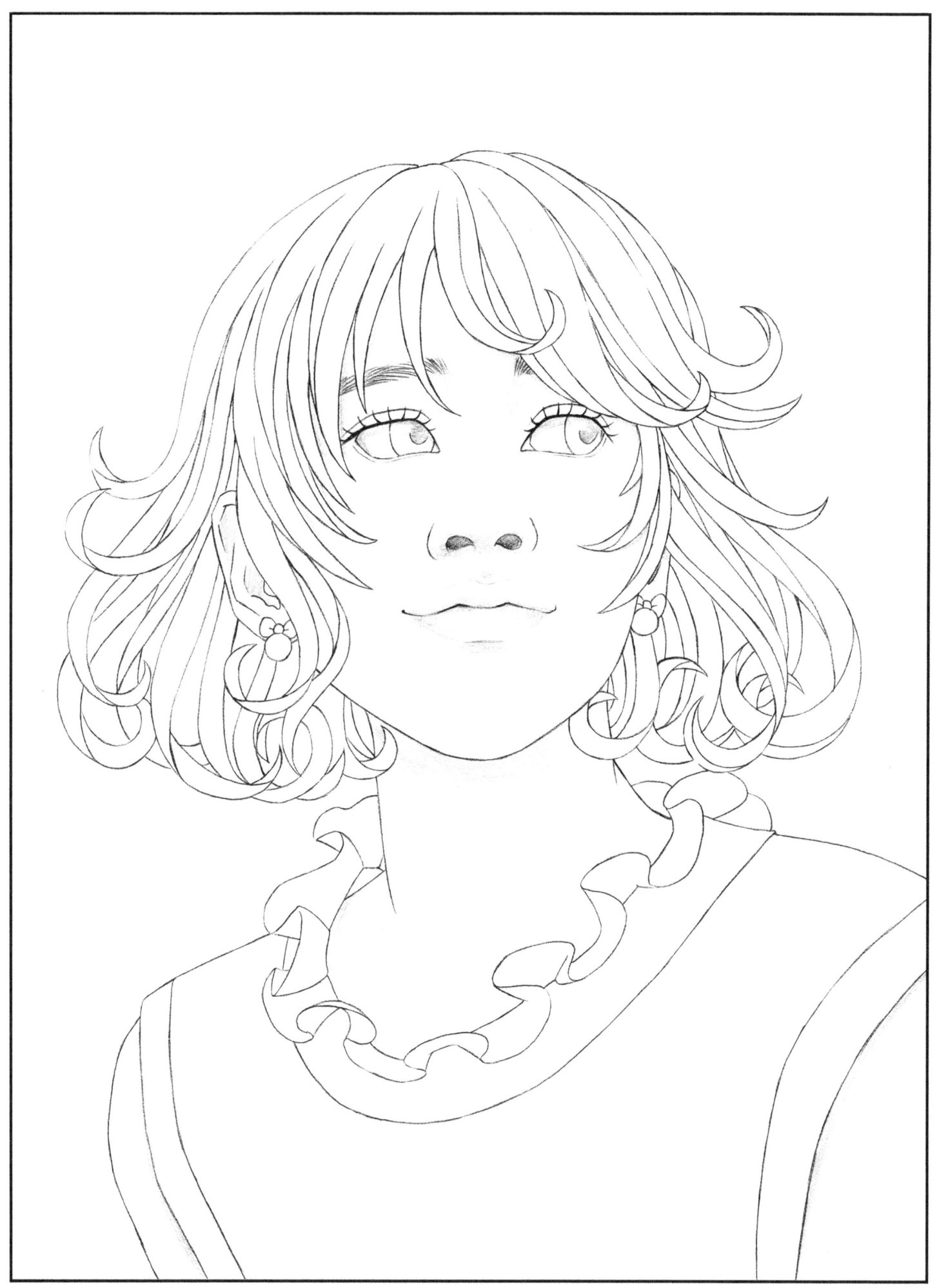

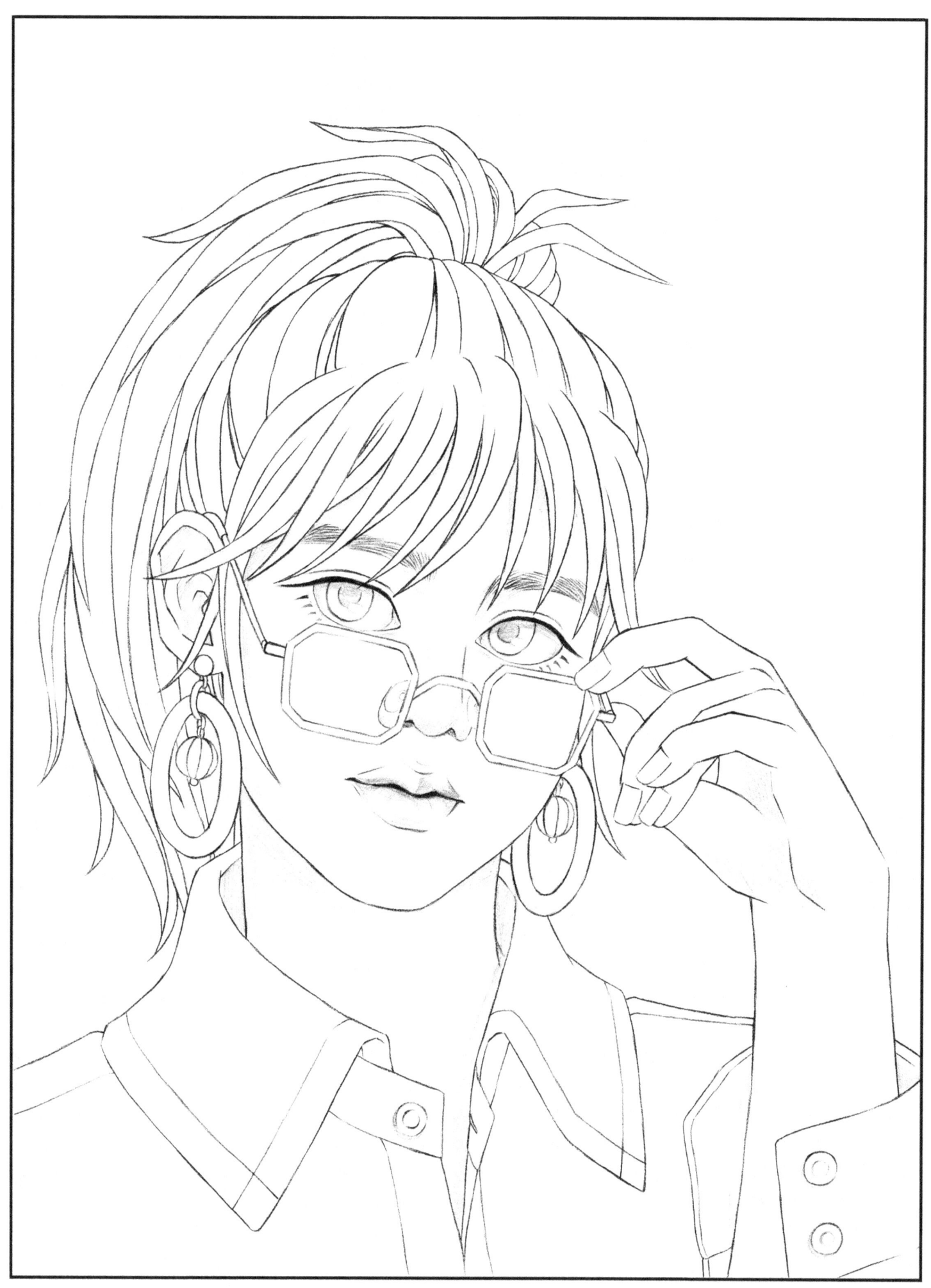

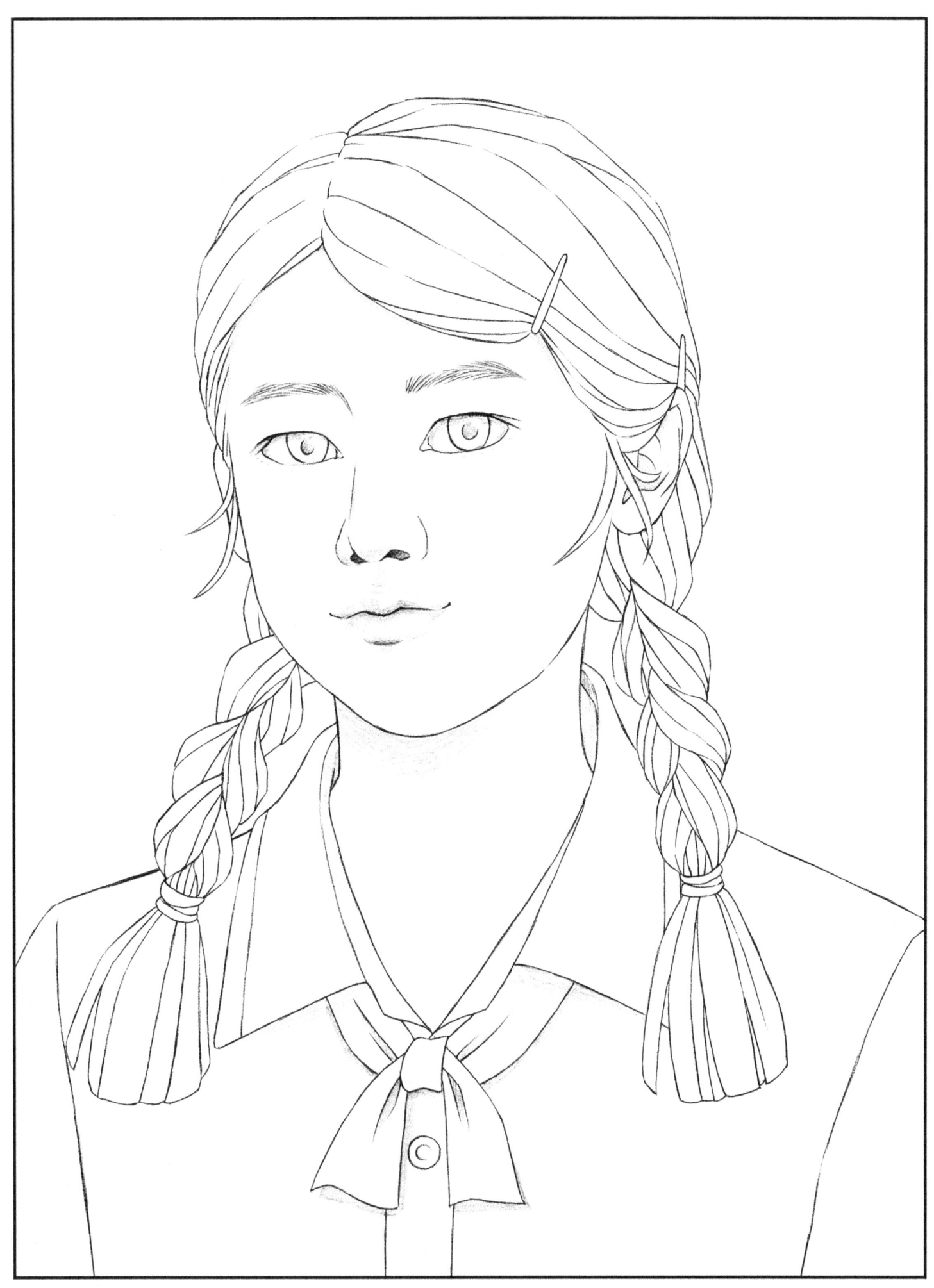

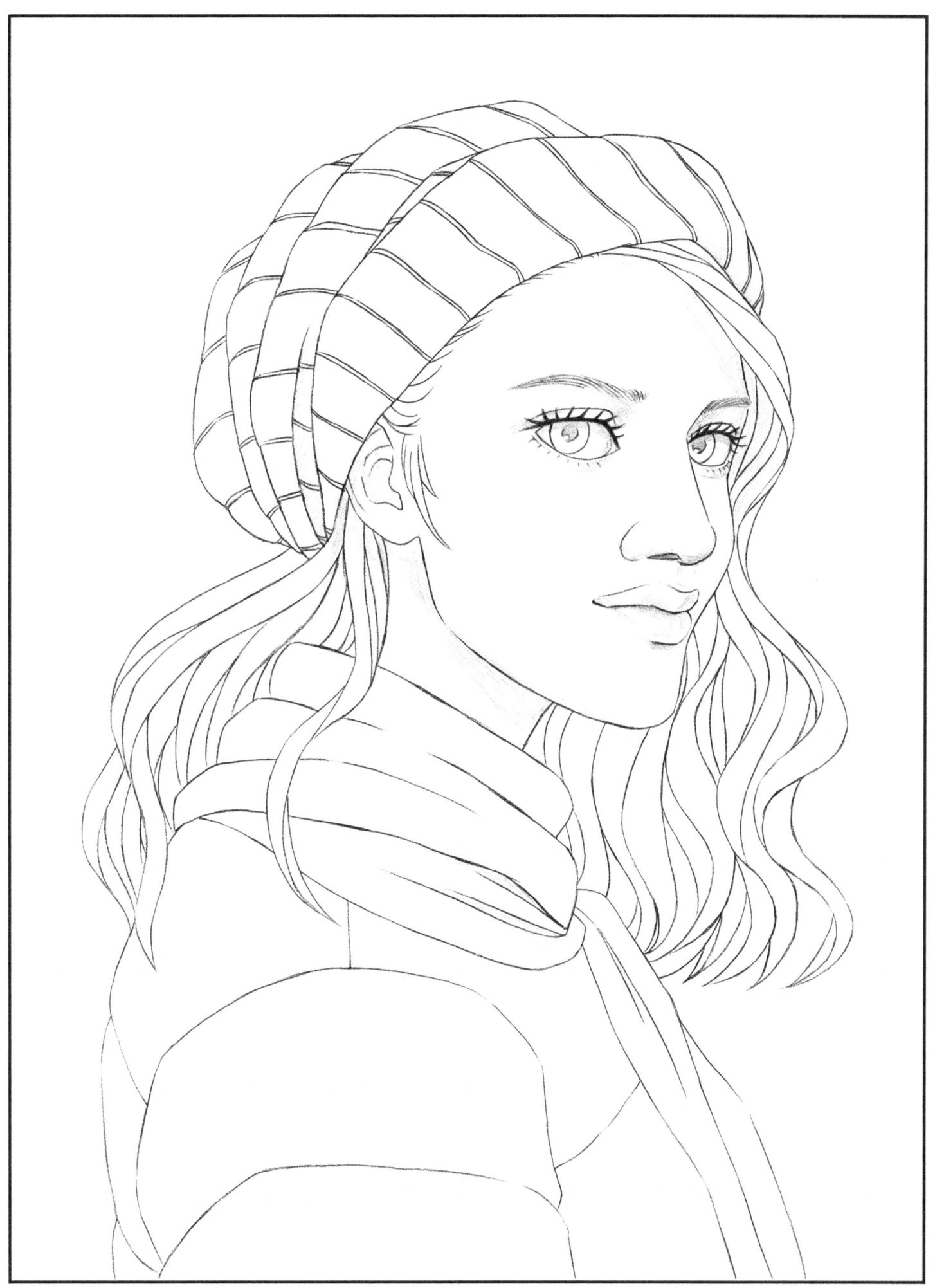

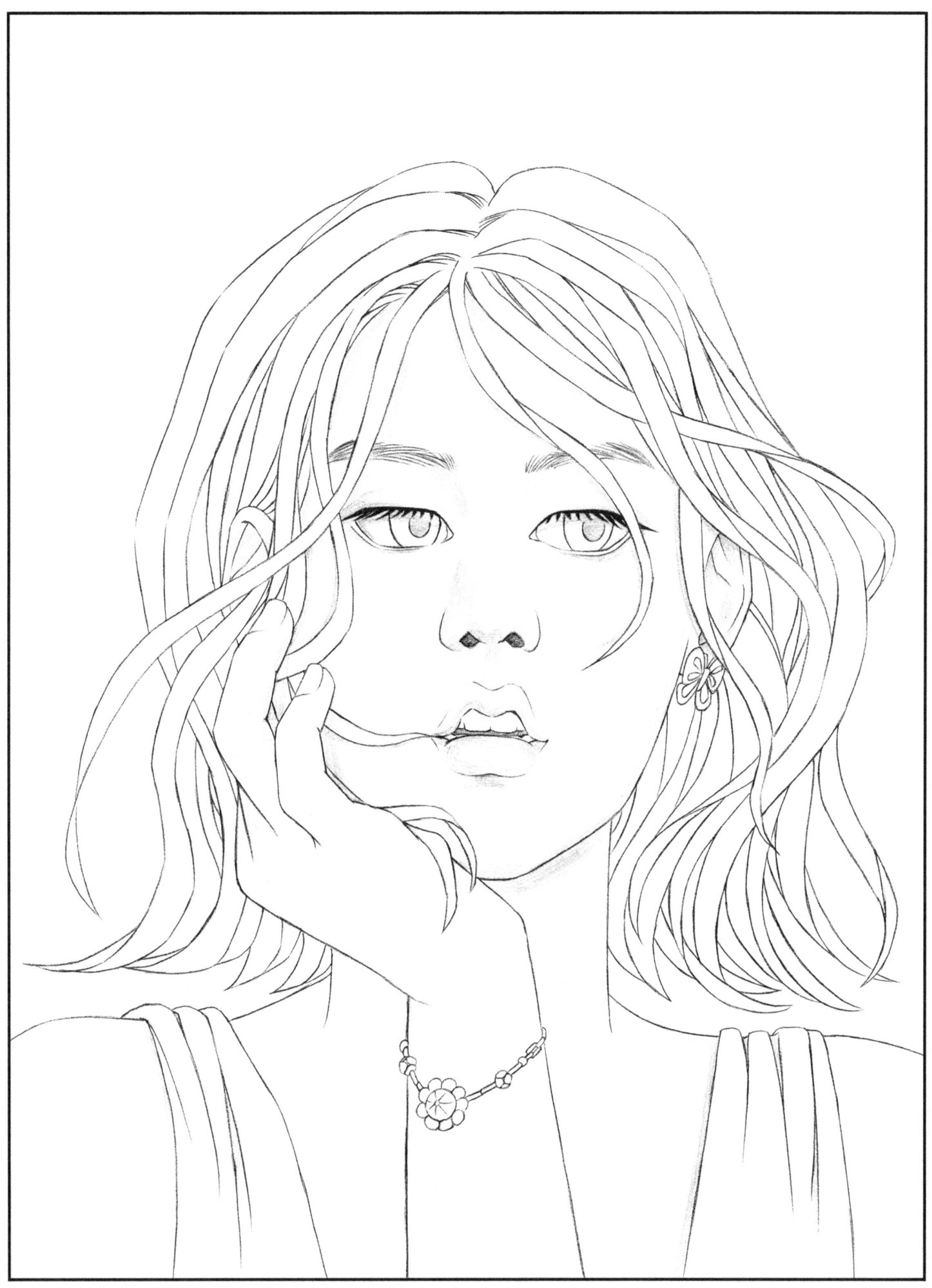

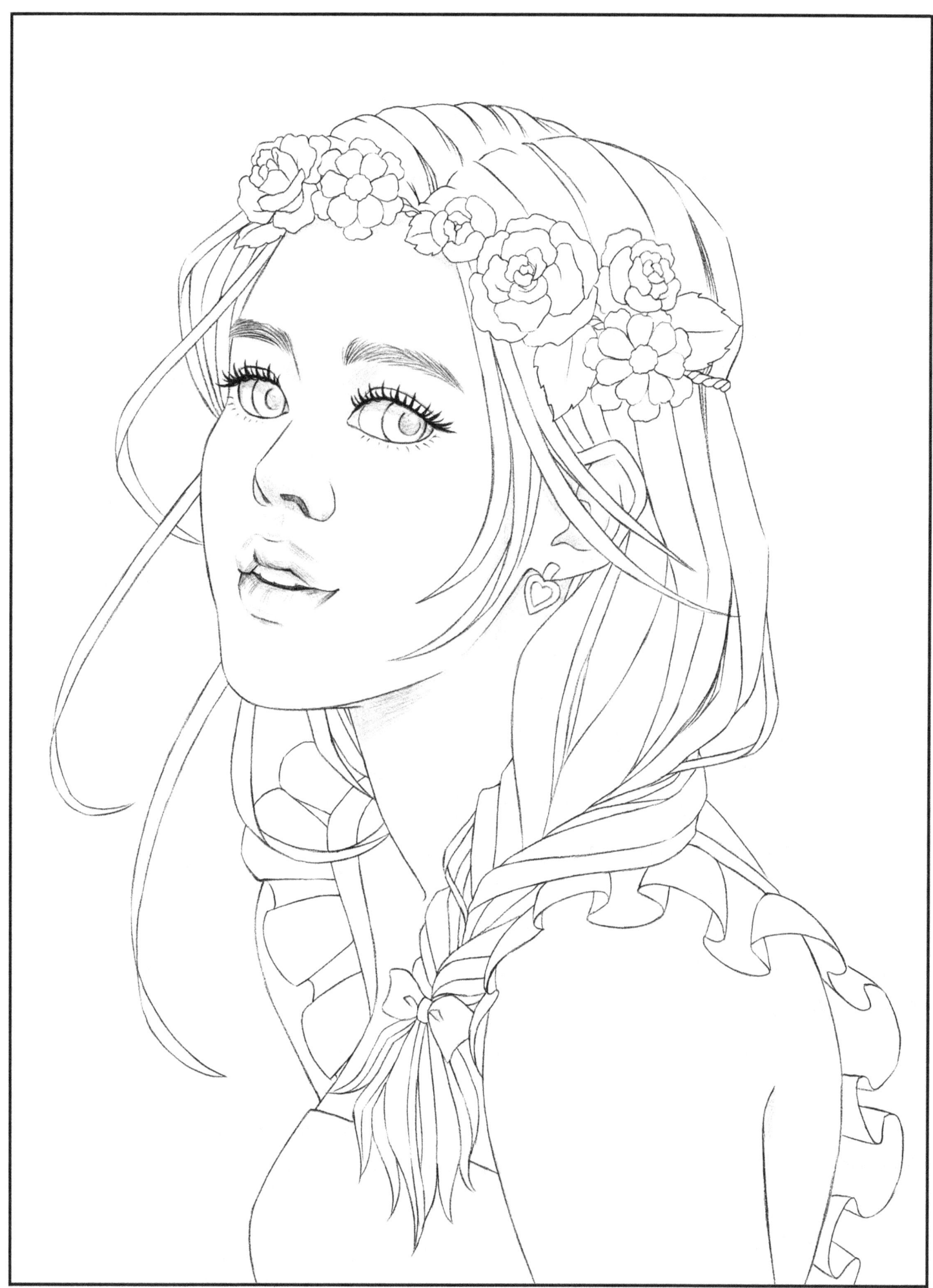

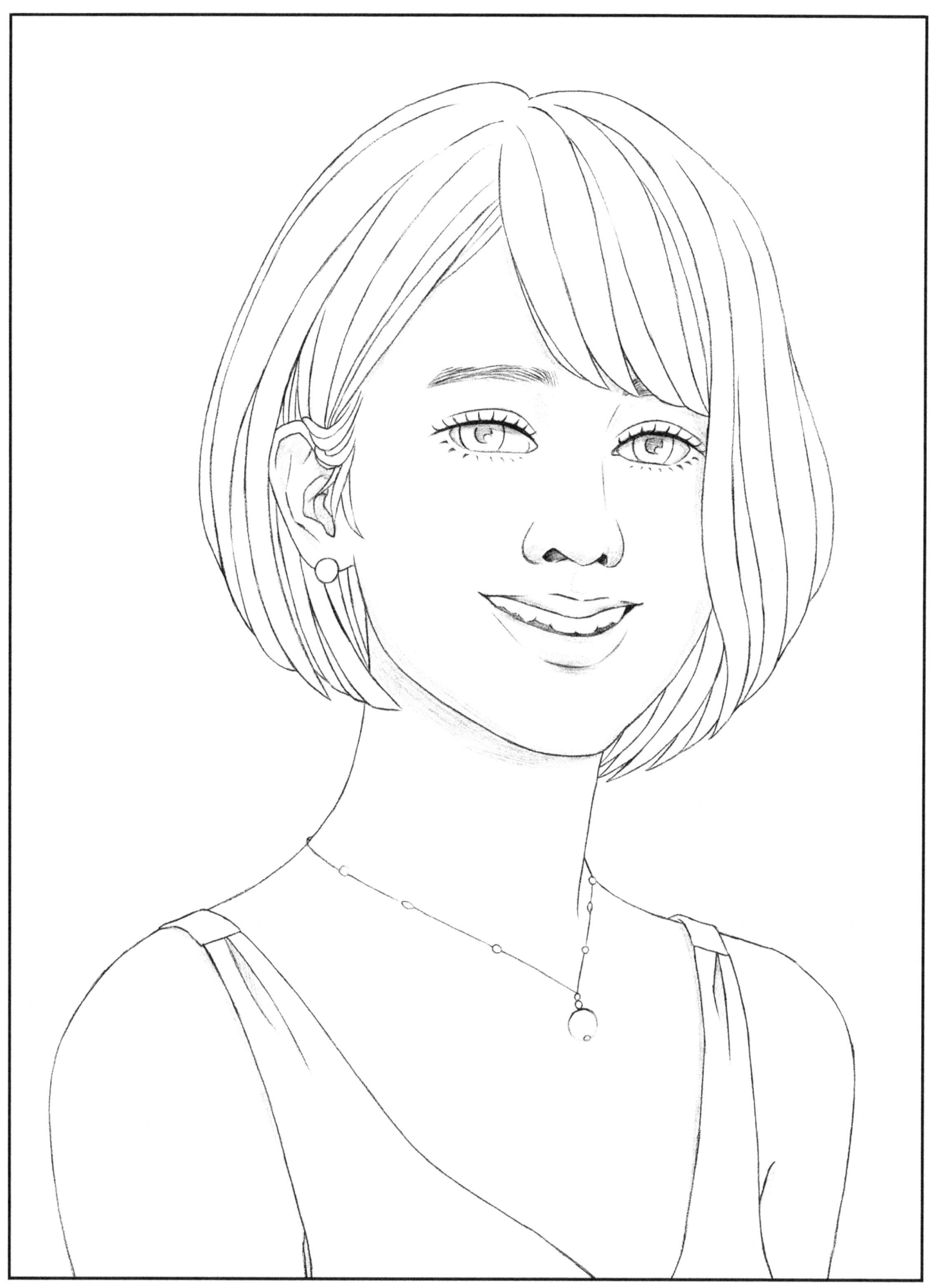

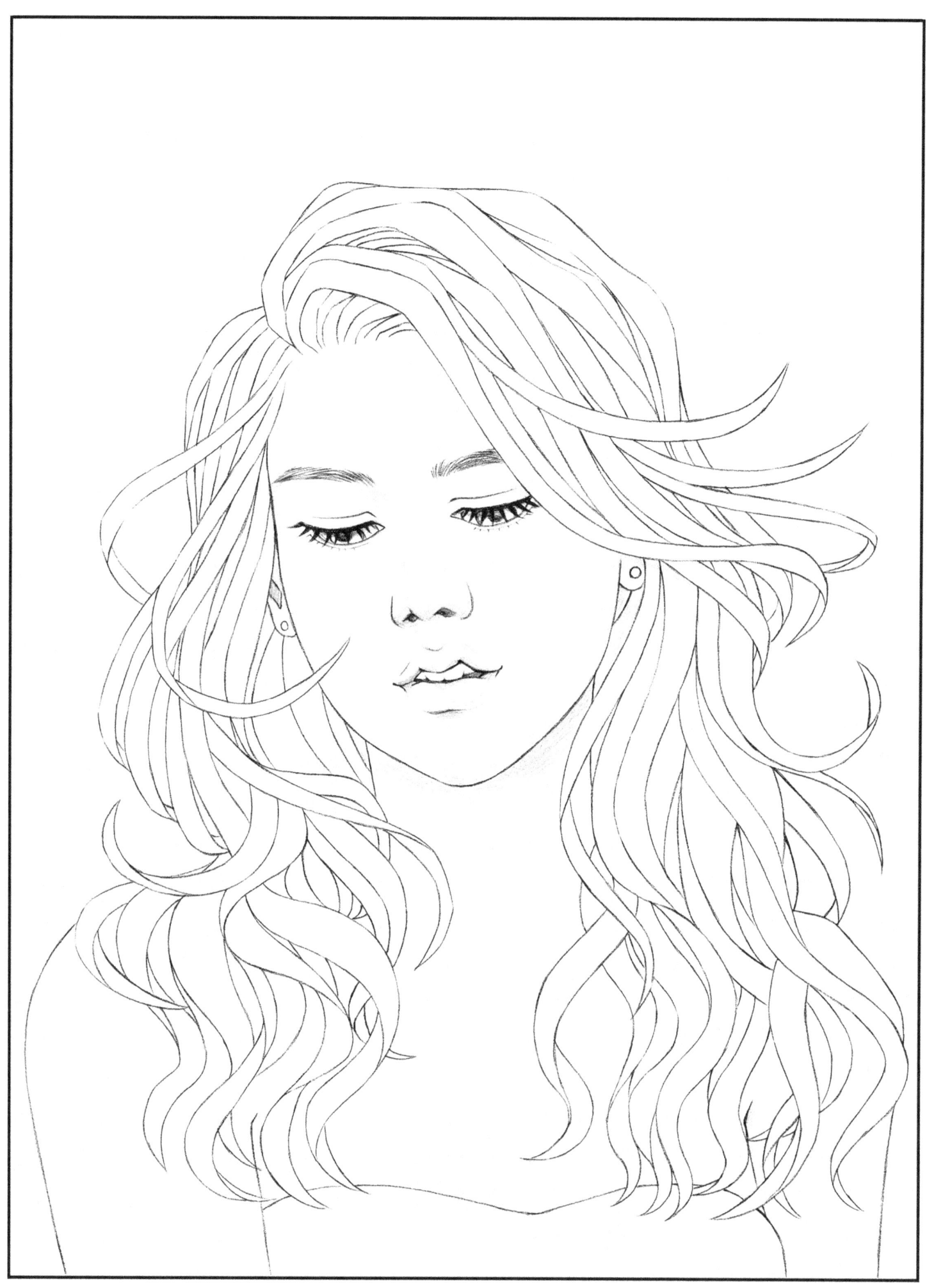

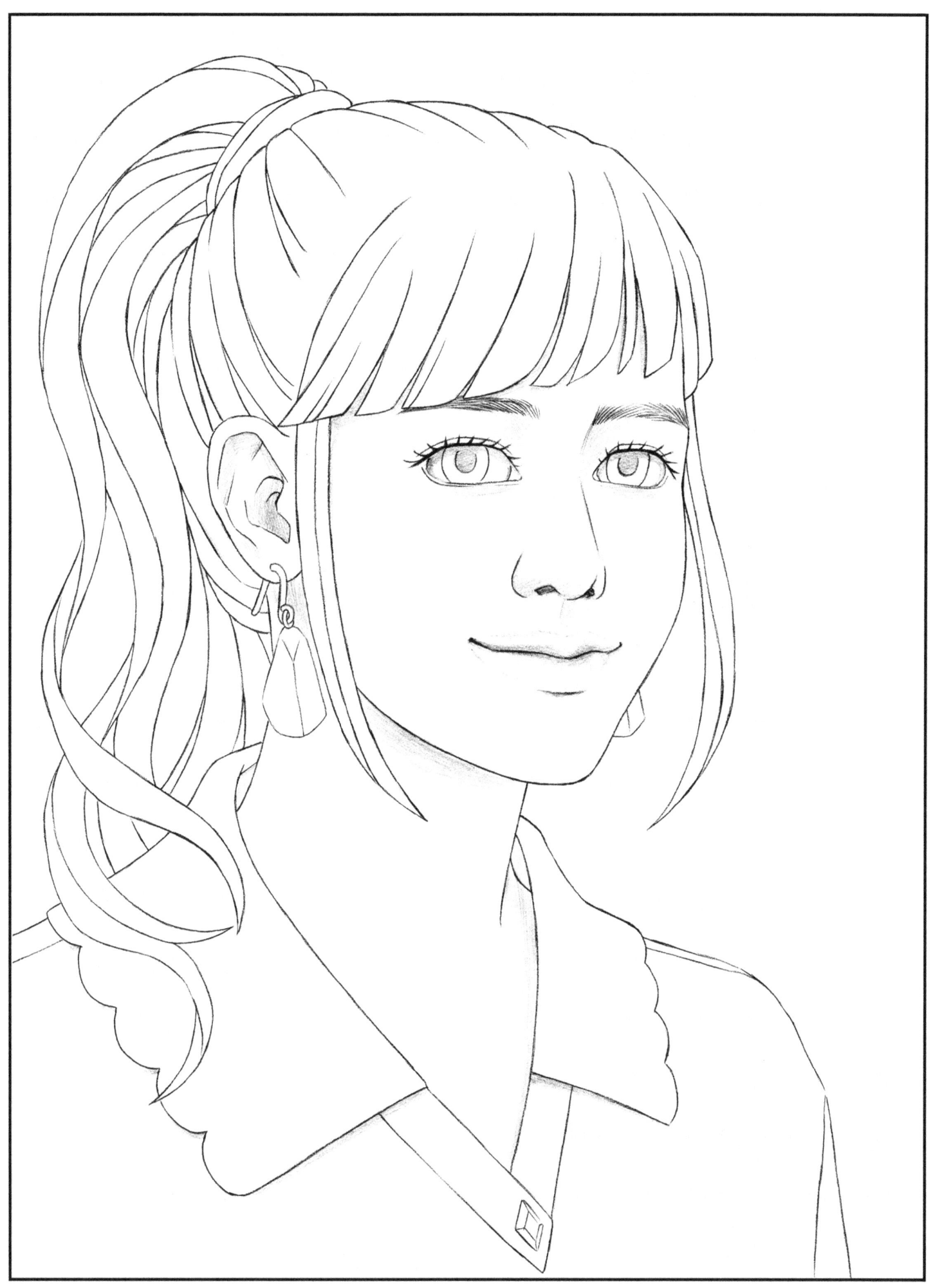

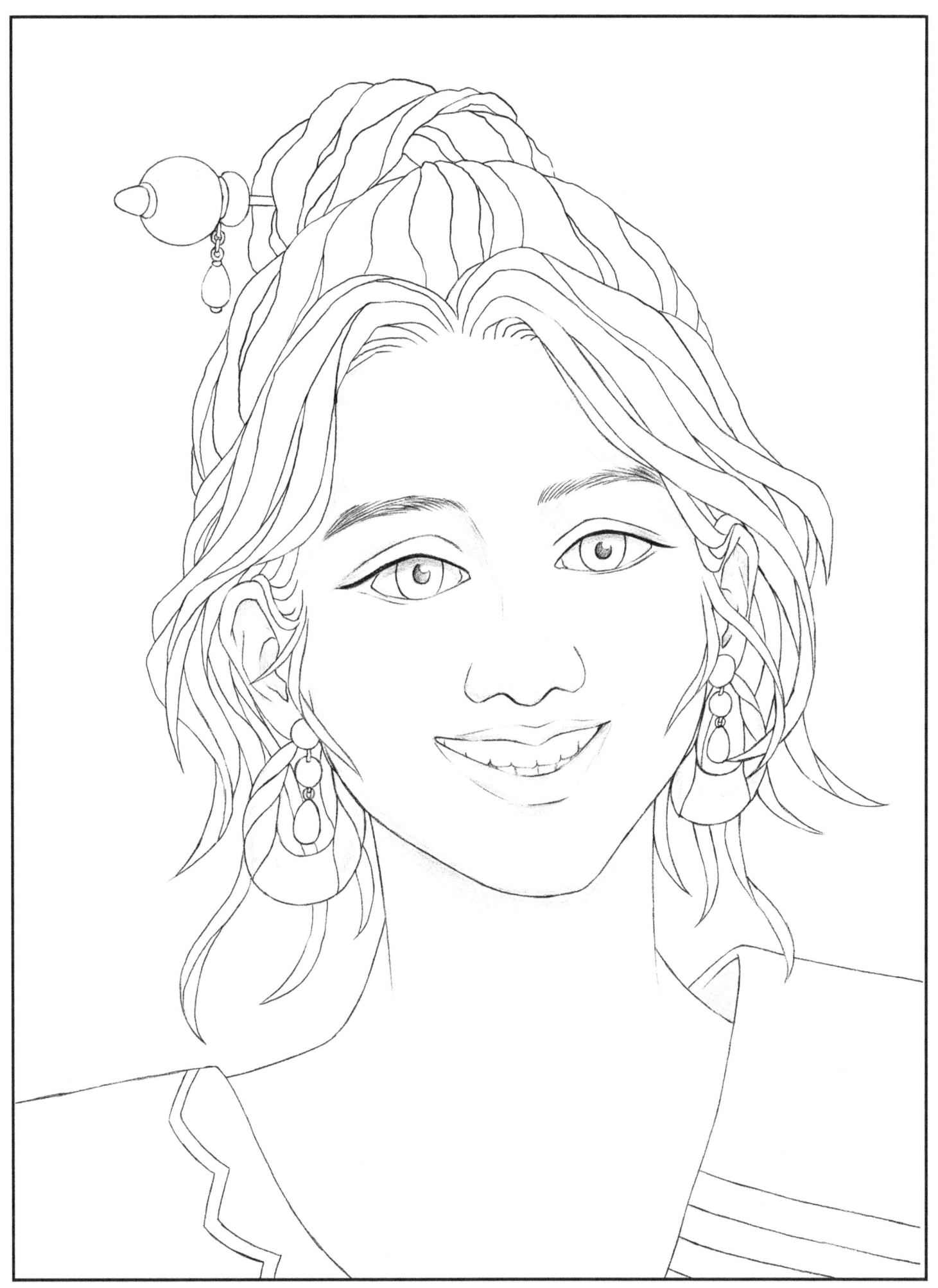

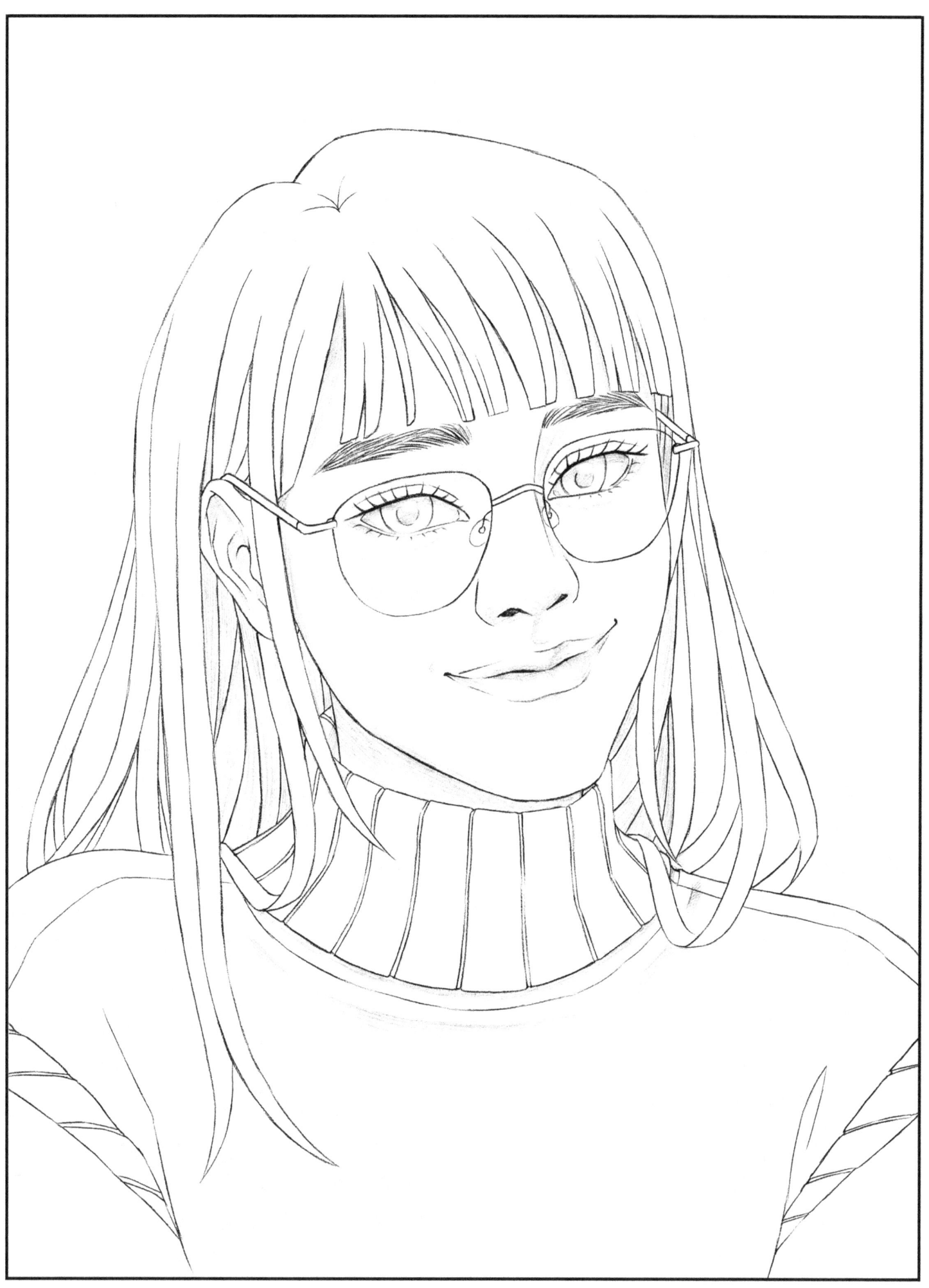

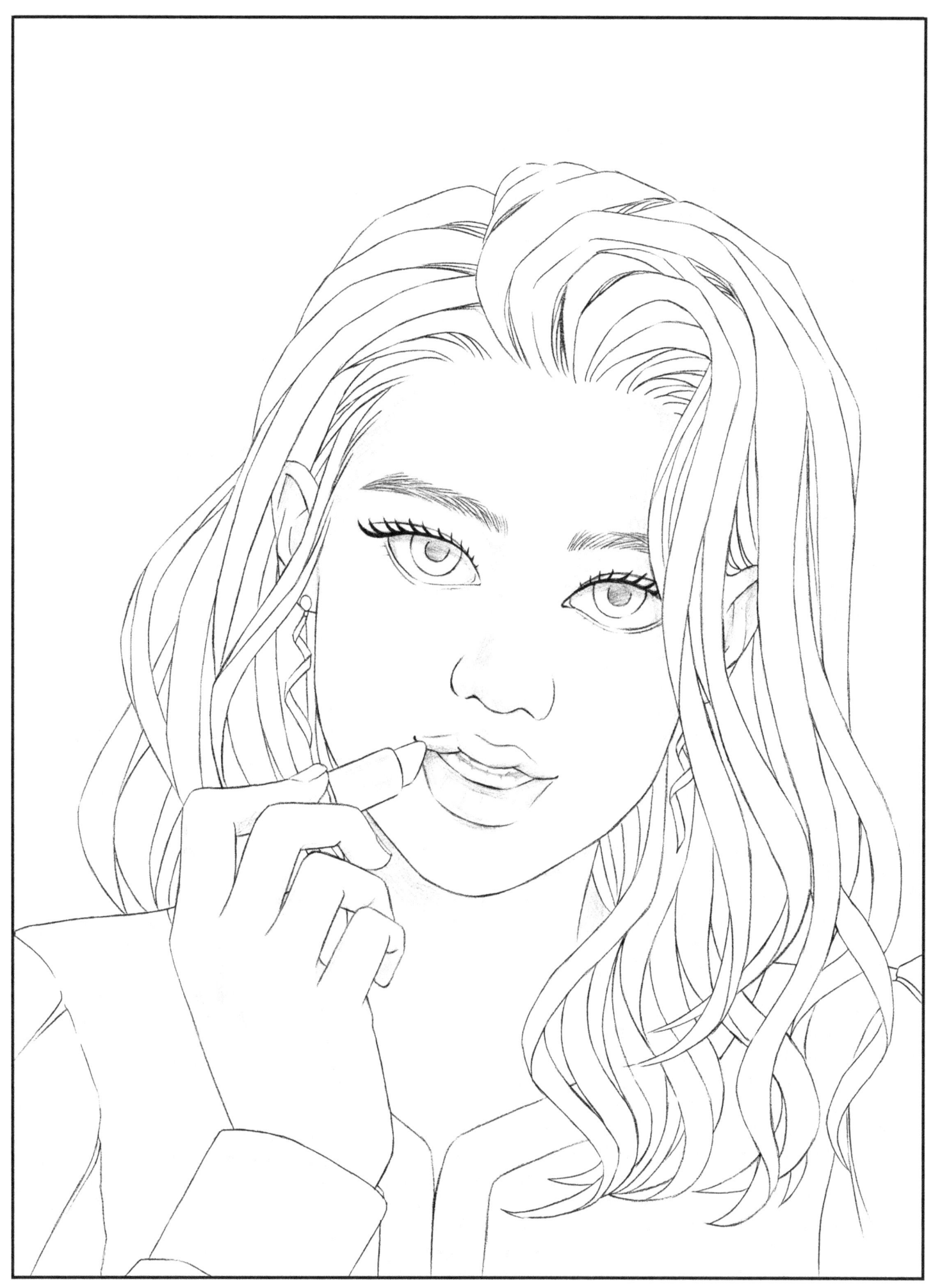

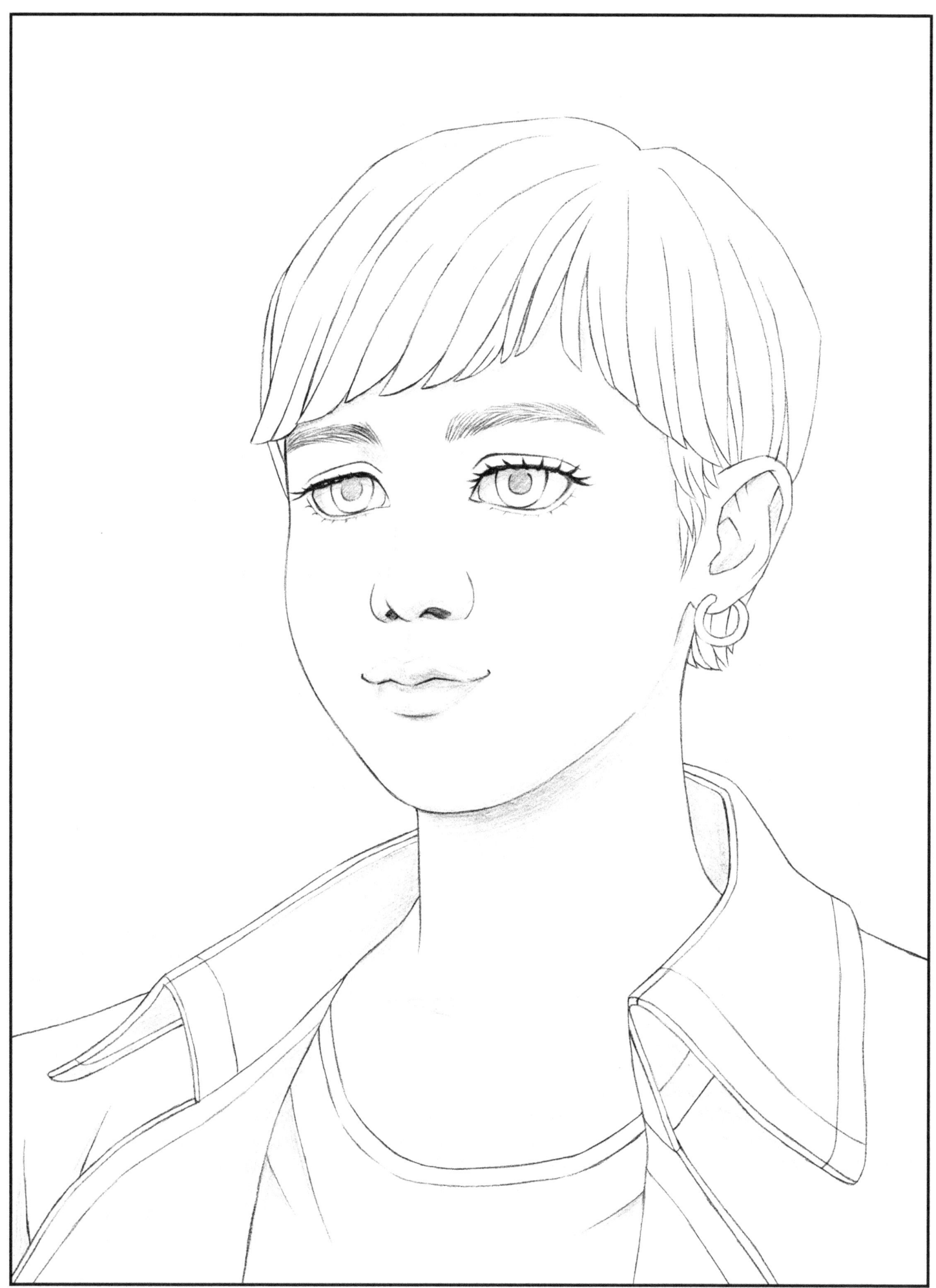

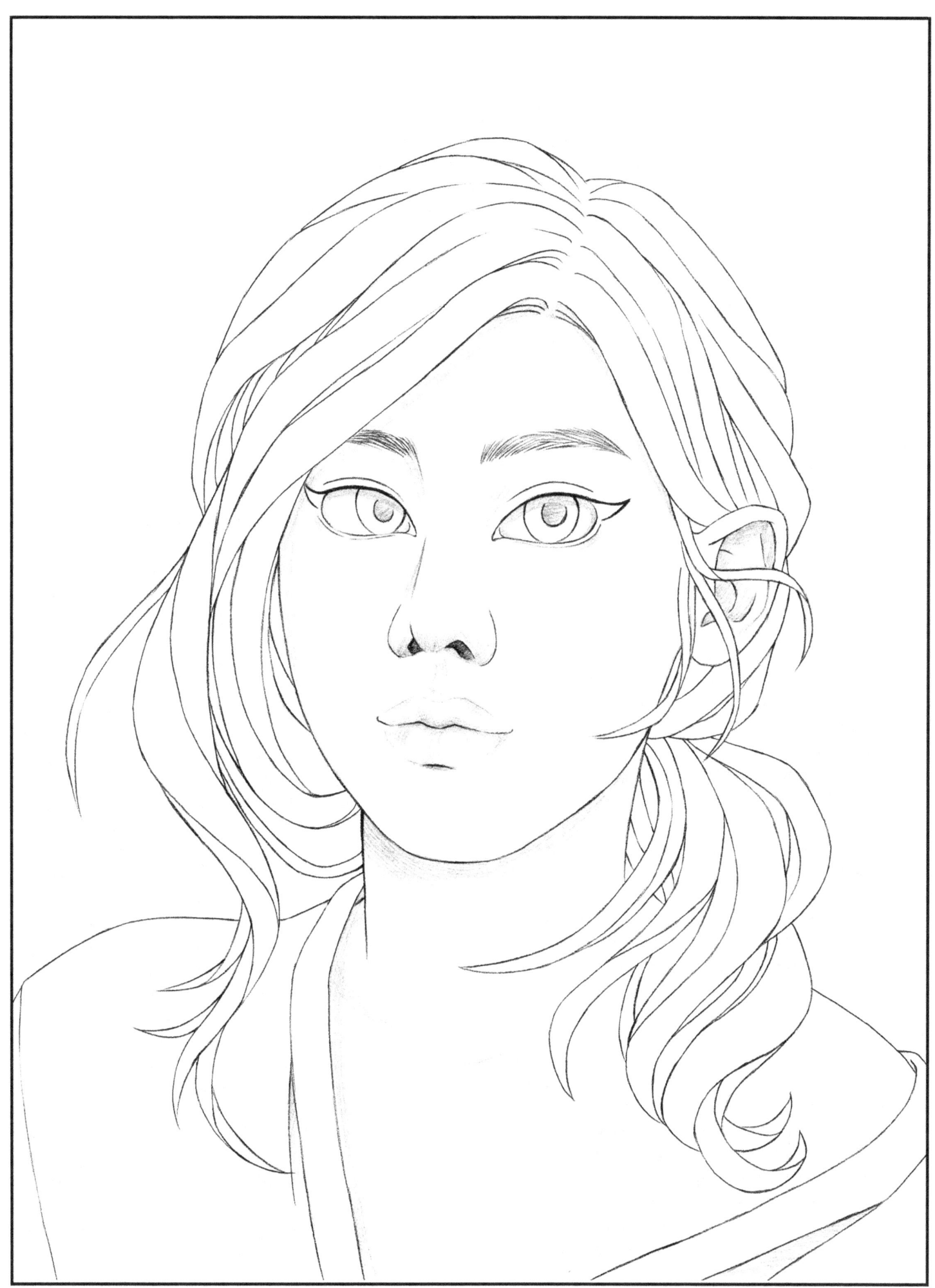

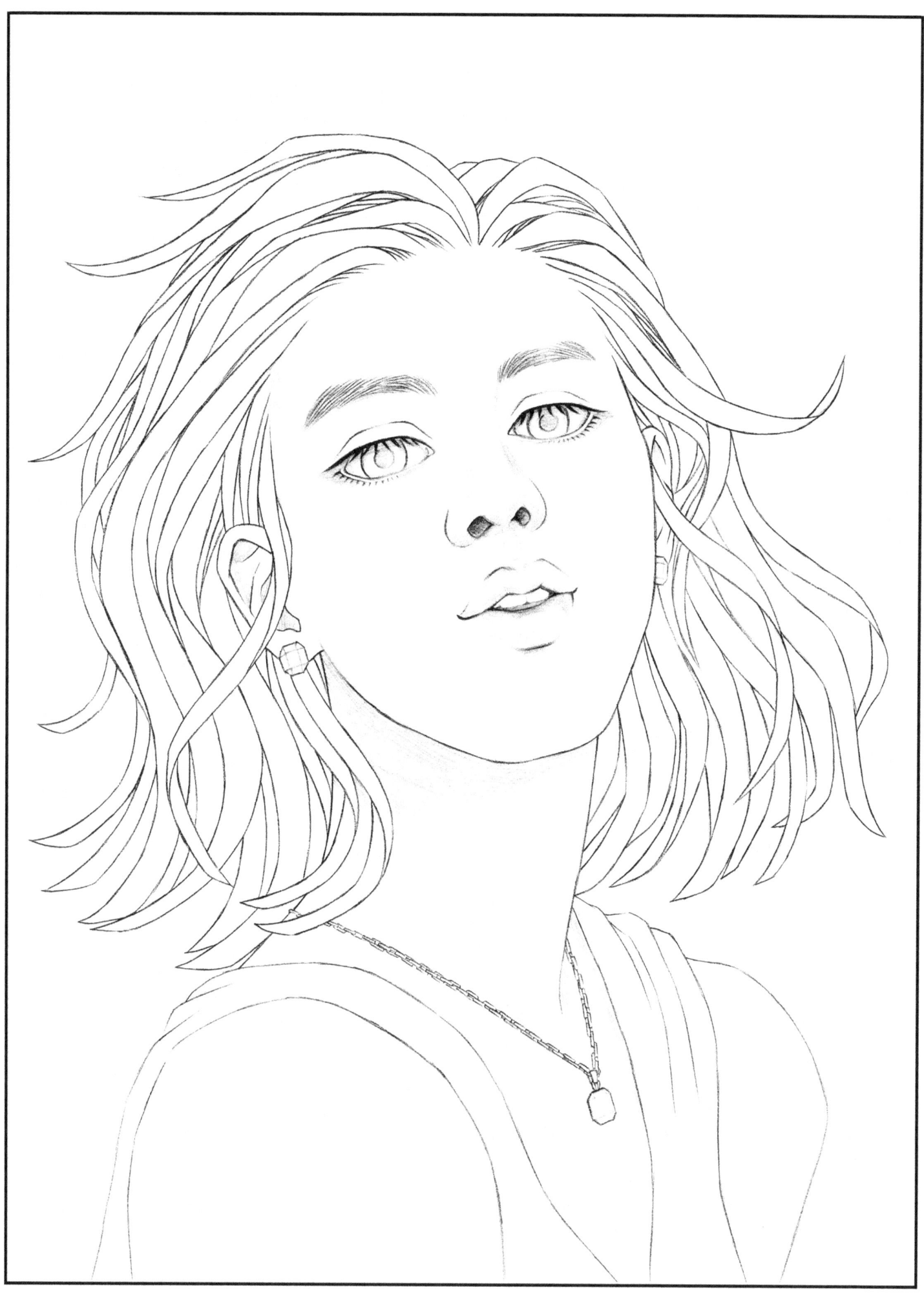

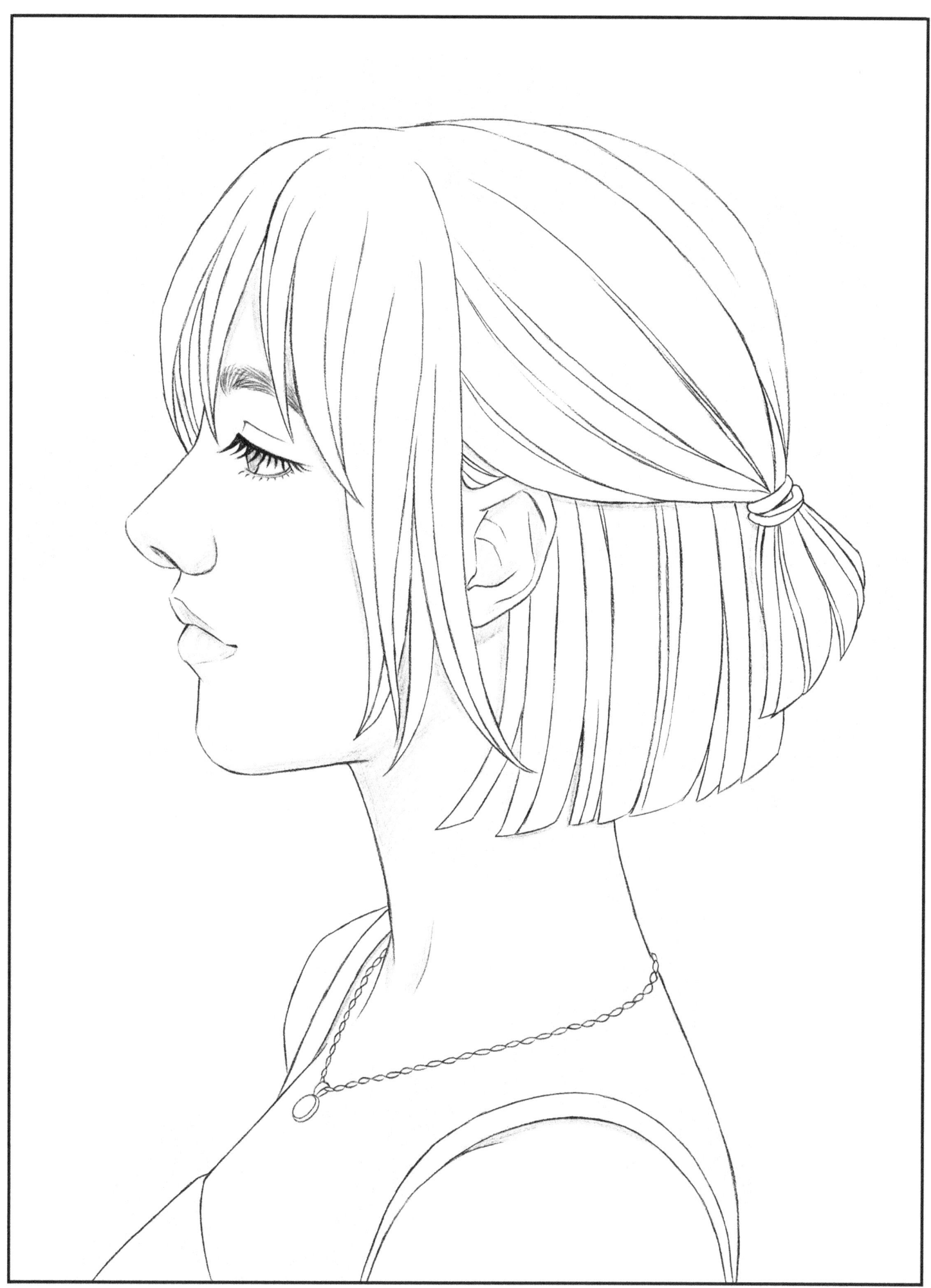

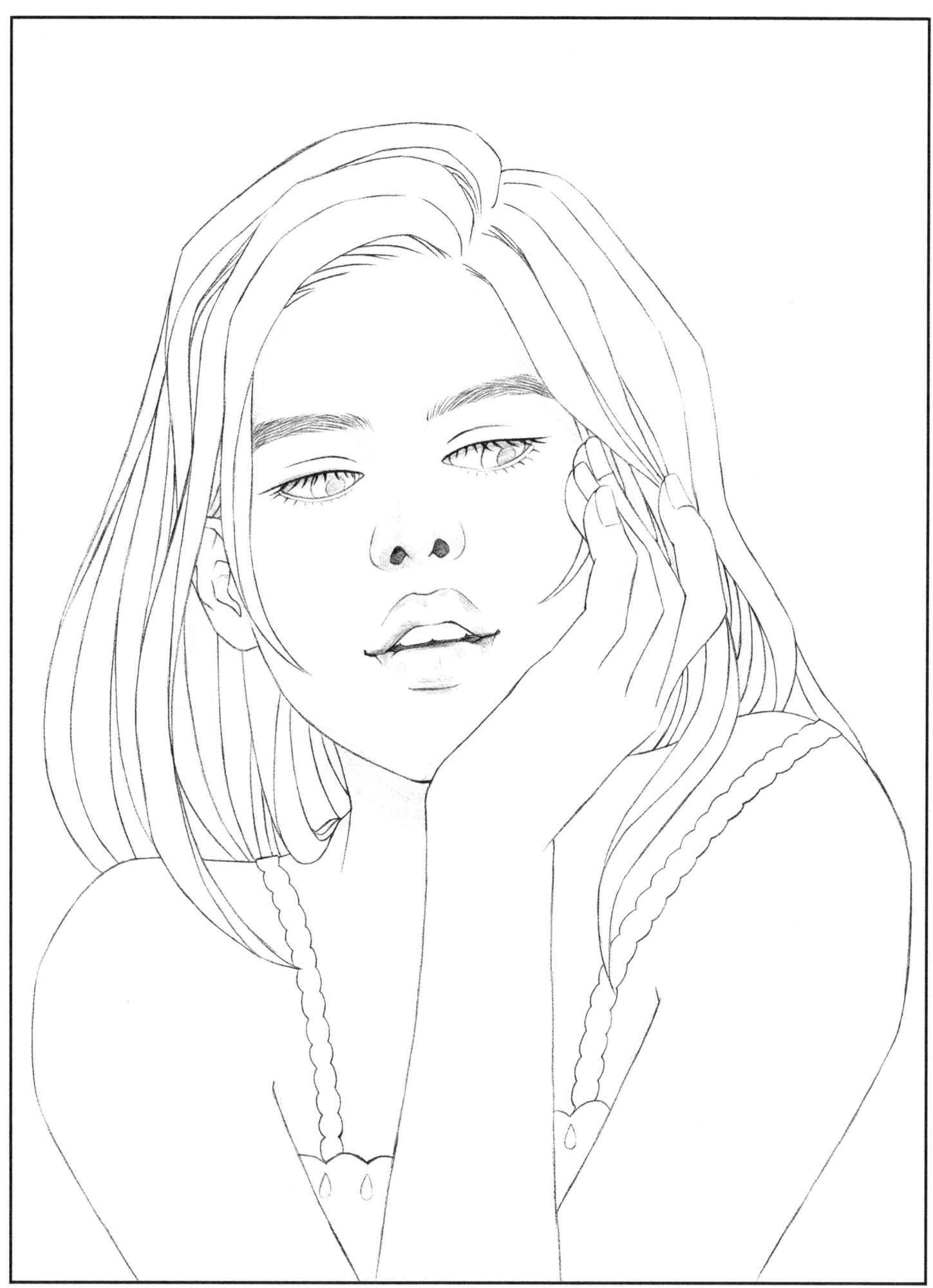

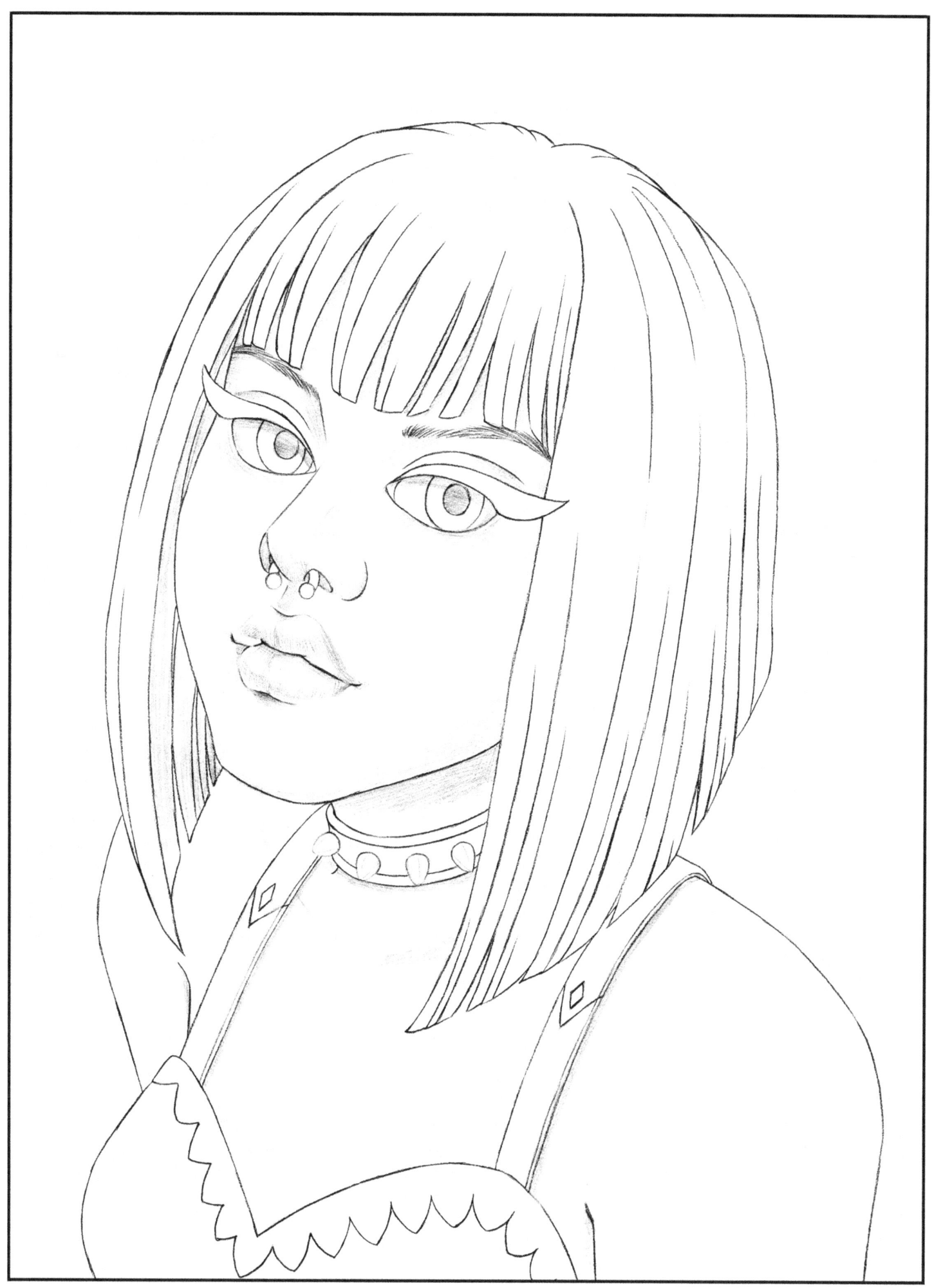

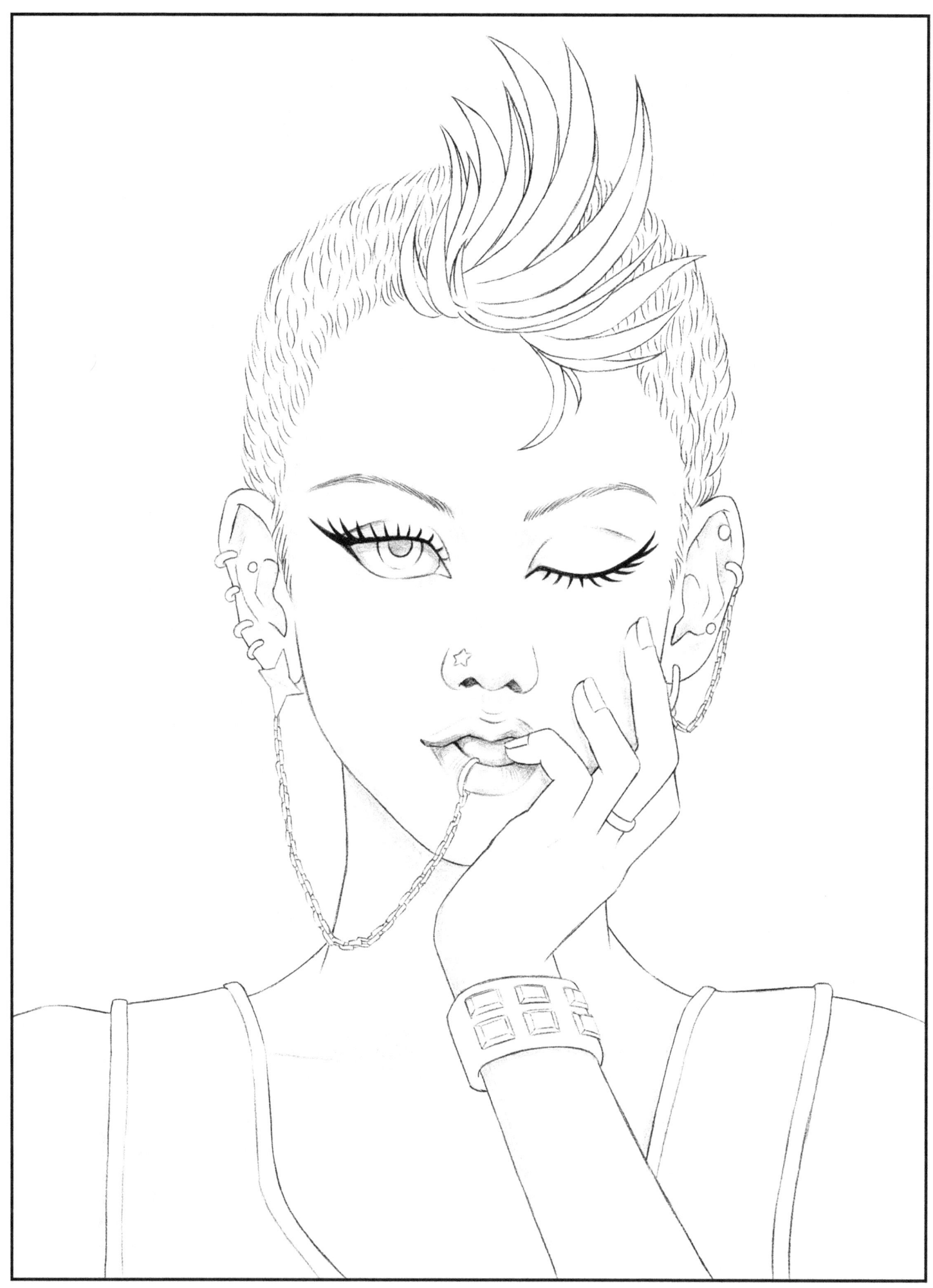

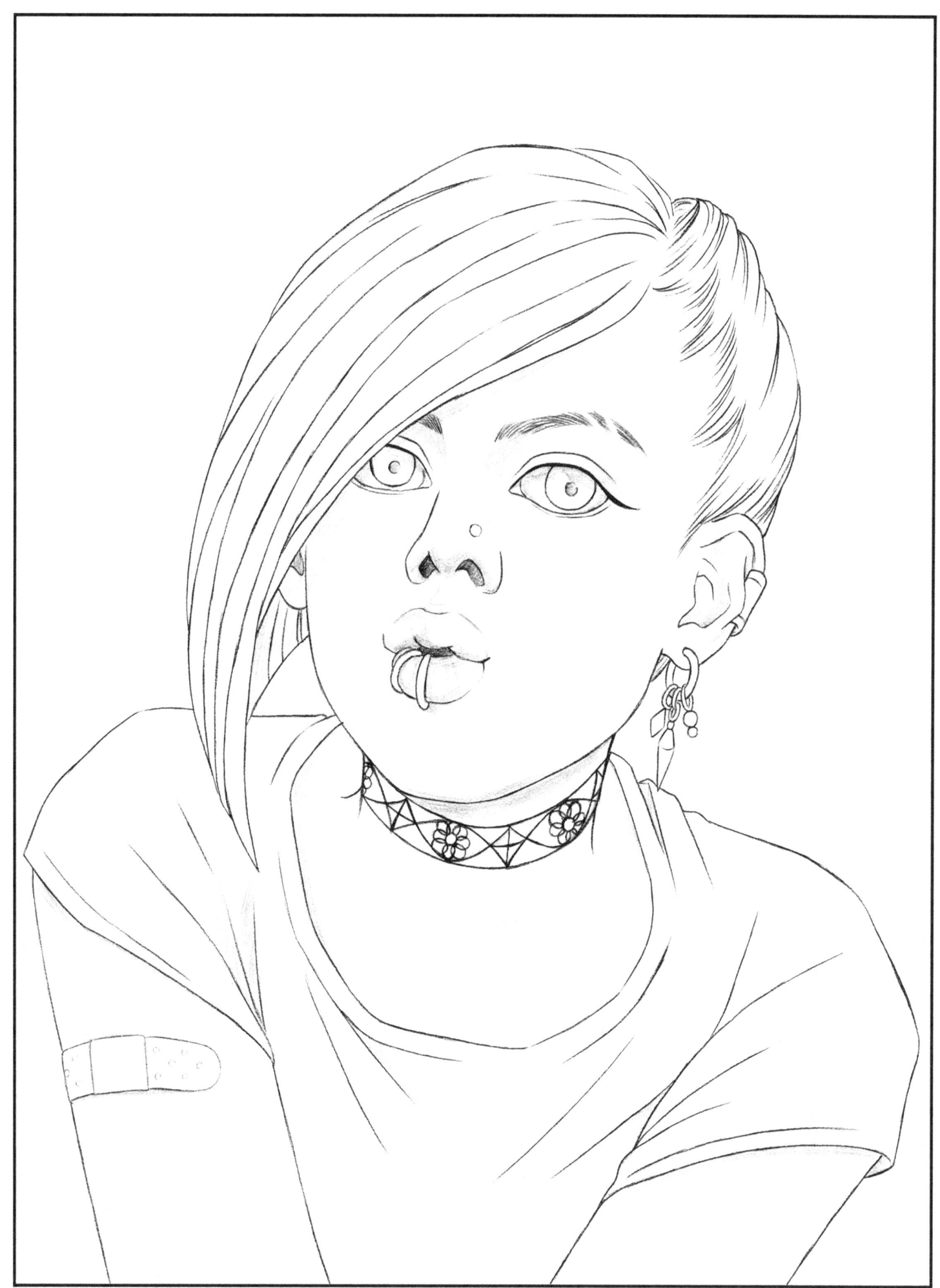

www.ingramcontent.com/pod-product-compliance
Lightning Source LLC
Chambersburg PA
CBHW081459220526
45466CB00008B/2707